D1569573

THE BASKETBALL COACH'S

GAME PLAN FOR

LEADERSHIP

**INTERVIEWS WITH BASKETBALL LEGENDS,
DETAILED PRACTICE PLANS, AND
COACHING STRATEGIES TO BUILD
YOUR TEAM'S LEADERSHIP CULTURE**

EDITED BY JOHN MADISON

**CHAMPIONSHIP
PERFORMANCE**

TABLE OF CONTENTS

Introduction and Foreword – Coach Eric Musselman

Section I: Fast Break Points – First Half

1. * Coach Implements Wooden Principles, * 'The Psyche' Pre-Game Ritual, * End Practice on a High Note, * Fifteen Core Values of USA Basketball, * Coaching Wisdom from Gail Goestenkors, * John Calipari Lets Shy Player Take Over Practice, * Eric Musselman on Motivation, * Bobby Hurley on Fantastic Finish, * Coach Dale's Motivation Speech, * Geno Auriemma's Tough Practices, * Coach K on Learning from Losses, * Pro Teams Embrace Technology, * Slowing Down a Force, * Pat Riley on Working Through Tough Times, * Rick Pitino's Pre-game Speech, * Billy Donovan on Video Motivation, * Bill Self on Final 4 Preparations, * Nate Macmillan's 3 C's of Timeouts, * Two Lessons from Coach K, * John Wooden's 10 Practice Reminders

Section II: Competition Tested Basketball Coaching Methods

2. SWAG Propels Gators to Final 4
3. Tom Crean on the Role of Assistant Coaches
4. Ben Howland's Defense First Philosophy
5. Anatomy of College Basketball's Greatest Upset
6. Denny Crum On Lessons Working with John Wooden
7. Bill Self Final 4 Pre-game Speech
8. Billy Donovan on Trying to Repeat a Championship
9. The Villanova Clutch Mind-set

Section VII: Fast Break Points – Second Half

FOREWORD — COACH ERIC MUSSELMAN

Over the past 30 years I have had the privilege of coaching at nearly every level possible, including youth basketball while coaching both of my son's teams. At each of those stops along the way I have learned a great deal that has helped mold and shape my philosophy into what it is today. I believe in hard work. That is the backbone of any successful organization, individual or program. But hard work must be purposeful. Hard work without a purpose gets you no-where. I have a specific routine in which I adhere to daily. Part of that routine includes a significant amount of reading. I do not just read to read. I am intentional about the material I read with the purpose of learning in order to apply some aspect of my learning to my program.

Learning from others successes and failures spurred my obsession with the material I read. You can learn from anyone and everyone, and those lessons add value to my program. When reading this book, the first thing I thought about was the great opportunity to have all these great coaches thoughts and philosophies put into one comprehensive leadership guide for young coaches to learn from. I got a chance to see first hand while working for my dad great leadership as well as several others that I got a chance to work for. The Basketball Coach's Game Plan for Leadership provides the tools for all young coaches who do not necessarily have those same opportunities.

Reading has been a staple of part of my coaching career. I read every single day and find new and interesting things to help motivate my team and my staff, new philosophies to implement and new ideas on X's and O's. There is not downside to reading this book. I believe the most successful people are those who can constantly adapt to the changing world. In today's game we all need to be up to date on how to motivate, what players like and don't like, how we can take lessons from the past and implement them in today's culture and how we as coaches can get the full potential out of each individual and each team. This book puts all those lessons and ideas from excellent coaches across the years into one comprehensive format for everyone to understand!

Eric Musselman

Eric Musselman is currently the Head Men's Basketball Coach at the University of Arkansas. His 30 plus year coaching career has included stops at the international, college and professional level with the University of Nevada, Golden State Warriors and Sacramento Kings and many others as an assistant coach. He has led his teams to two Sweet Sixteens and one Elite 8 appearance and three Mountain West titles.

University of Kentucky head coach John Calipari said this about Coach Musselman: "Eric is one of the best in our sport. He is extremely driven and knowledgeable. I've watched and coached against him in the NBA and FIBA games. He has an uncanny feel for the game, and ability to read where the game is at during a given point in time. More importantly, is his ability to motivate and teach his players what it takes to improve and win. He is as good as it gets."

SECTION I

Fast Break Points — First Half

1. ● Coach Implements Wooden Principles

After a losing season, a high school basketball coach decided to implement some of Coach John Wooden's practice rules. The positive impact was immediate. He made the following changes:
1) Never extending a practice beyond its scheduled time. 2) Never having practice go beyond two hours. 3) Limit each practice activity to eight minutes. 4) Integrate water breaks between conditioning drills. 5) Cut down transition time between practice activities by distributing detailed written practice plans to assistant coaches so that everyone would know where and when to place equipment needed for each activity.

● 'The Psych' Pre-Game Ritual

One coach uses her athlete profiles to pair two players together and have them tell a pre-game story called "the Psych." Throughout the season, two players must come up with a brief story to tell their teammates in the locker before games. The talks can come in the form of a poem, personal thought, or a prop that represents the message.

● End Practice on a High Note

Two-time national coach of the year Charles "Chuck" Kyle used this strategy to end his practices on a high note. He created a ten second tradition at the end of every practice for each player to visualize himself correcting an error he had made in that day's practice. The goal was for each athlete to leave the practice with a positive image of himself performing successfully.

• Fifteen Core Values of US Basketball

When Duke Basketball Coach K took over the Olympic team, he came up with 15 core values for the team. Here is the list: 1) No excuses. We have what it takes to win. 2) Great defense. This is the key to winning gold, so we do the dirty work. 3) Communication. We look each other in the eye and tell each other the truth. 4) Trust. We believe in each other. 5) Collective responsibility. We are committed to each other and we win together. 6) Care. We have each other's backs and we give aid to teammates. 7) Respect. We respect each other and our opponents. We are always on time and always prepared. 8) Intelligence. We take good shots, we're aware of team fouls, and we know the scouting report. 9) Poise. We don't show weakness. 10) Flexibility. We can handle any situation without complaints. 11) Unselfishness. We're connected. We make the extra pass and our value to our team is not measured in playing time. 12) Aggressiveness. We play hard every possession. 13) Enthusiasm. This is fun. 14) Performance. We're hungry. 15) Pride. We are the best team in the world and we represent the best country.

• Coaching Wisdom from Gail Goestenkors

NCAA and WNBA basketball coach Gail Goestenkors offers these nuggets of coaching wisdom:

• Duke has a buddy system where players are paired up, usually a reserve with a starter. During time-outs, the buddy not playing provides a drink and encouragement to her partner. To prepare players how to act on the bench, the Duke coaches demonstrate how to be supportive, including cheers and the best way to high five.

• Players contribute to scouting reports, watching tape with coaches and writing down the strengths and weakness of opponents. They also have a practice player of the day and year, based on hustle and fundamentals.

• Roles are generally accepted by players for the good of the team. One player commented: "We always talk about how knowing your role is so important. Although some of us would like bigger roles sometimes, we need to perfect the ones we have, especially during tournament time. It helps us to hold each other accountable."

● Calipari Let Shy Player Take Over Practice

While coaching at Memphis, John Calipari turned over practice to forward Robert Dozier in a move designed to force the quiet senior to take more of a leadership role with the team.

To make the impact of the change of practice pace more meaningful, Calipari left the gym, leaving Dozier on his own to coach. He told Dozier: "It's your team now for the rest of practice."

"He thought I was too quiet," Dozier recalled. "He wanted me to be vocal, get on guys and be more of a leader. I was mad at first, because I didn't want to do it. But I had fun with it. The guys enjoyed it. It wasn't a long practice."

The usually subdued Dozier said he tried to get as animated as Calipari, a dynamic, demonstrative speechmaker never at a loss for words. "I had to tone it down," Dozier said, laughing. "There were a lot of people in there."

• Eric Musselman on Motivation

College and NBA coach Eric Musselman is known for his motivational prowess. In an effort to create a positive setting with one of his teams, he once changed the locker colors from blue to gold and the lights from dim to bright. You have to start with small steps to change a team's direction.

He once helped his former team, the Atlanta Hawks, do well in a rematch with the Orlando Magic. After the Magic defeated the Hawks by 34, Magic star Tracy McGrady called the Hawks a "cupcake."

Musselman printed the story, made copies for the team and wrote "CUPCAKE" on the team's locker room chalkboard. The Hawks won the game the following night.

• Hurley Reflects on Fantastic Finish

With 2.1 seconds left in double overtime, Duke faced a defining moment. In one of the greatest NCAA tournament games ever played, the team sat on the bench eagerly awaiting instructions from their leader—Coach Mike Krzyzewski.

According to former Duke point guard and now college coach Bobby Hurley: "I remember thinking our season was over. We came back to the team huddle after Kentucky took the lead. Coach K came in and grabbed everyone's attention in that huddle.

He said, 'We're going to win this game.'

He asked Grant Hill if he could make a full court pass. Grant said 'Yes'. He asked Christian if he could make the shot. He said 'Yes.'

He made everyone believe it (the game winning shot) before it actually happened."

• Coach Dale's Motivation Speech

In the fictional high school basketball drama Hoosiers, the coach of the team gives a play-off pre-game pep talk: "There's a tradition in tournament play to not talk about the next step until you've climbed the one in front of you. I'm sure going to the State finals is beyond your wildest dreams, so let's just keep it right there.

Forget about the crowds, the size of the school, their fancy uniforms, and remember what got you here. Focus on the fundamentals that we've gone over time and time again.

And most important, don't get caught up thinking about winning or losing this game. If you put your effort and concentration into playing to your potential, to be the best that you can be, I don't care what the scoreboard says at the end of the game, in my book we're gonna be winners!

Okay?! [Players begin to clap in unison]

Alright let's go!"

• Geno Auriemma's Tough Practice

Few coaches are fixated on fouls like Connecticut women's basketball coach Geno Auriemma. Former players can recite his mantra: "Great players don't foul."

Sue Bird, a Seattle Storm guard who played for UCONN, said avoiding fouls reflects "an underlying theme" of Auriemma's coaching: "Good players don't put themselves in bad positions."

When a team plays right, "you're the one dictating the action," Bird said. "A lot of fouls are caused by being the one that's reacting to the scenario, rather than dictating it."

Smart defense is a perennial focus of Auriemma's practices, current and former players said. Former Connecticut star Breanna Stewart recalled one drill, a one-on-one matchup in which the defender has to stop the drive in order to "get out" and join her teammates. In an early practice, Stewart said, "I couldn't get a stop. And when I thought I got a stop, Coach called a foul: 'Go Again! Go Again!'" she said. "I couldn't get off the court."

Rebecca Lobo, an ESPN analyst who won a national championship with Connecticut, was watching that practice – she called it "brutal" and remembered doing the drill herself. While some coaches might let teammates "kill each other" in the service of making the team tougher, Lobo said, Auriemma and his assistants help "players learn how to be tough, but they don't do it while teaching bad habits on the defensive end of the floor."

• Coach K on Learning from Losses

For Duke's Coach K, losses have as much to do with his unprecedented success as his victories: "One thing that has never changed for me as a coach is that I hate to lose. But losses are inevitable. You don't want them to be a repeated act. You have to be honest about why you lost, whether it's lack of preparation, lack of energy or enthusiasm, or a loss of competitiveness. If you don't see losses as part of the growth process, they will become part of the destructive process."

• Pro Teams Embrace Technology

NBA basketball coach Alvin Gentry passes around a tablet computer during time-outs. The tablets are equipped with game video and customized scouting reports. Gentry said the tablets are the best way to show play diagrams he wants to run because he can attach a video to them, thanks to the assistant coach Noel Gillespie, the team's video coordinator. If Gentry tells Gillespie that he wants to run a play called "4 pop," Gillespie can cue the play right up for the entire team to view.

• Slowing Down a Force

When she was in college, Baylor's 6'8" Brittney Griner was a force to be reckoned with. Here are a couple of methods teams used to prepare for her:

• Coach Kim Barnes-Arico: "We used brooms to simulate her length and wing-span and to alter shots and distract our players on

Success is the peace of mind that comes from knowing you gave the best effort you were capable of giving.

JOHN WOODEN

the offensive end. On the defensive end, we changed our whole scheme. We had somebody face guard her and put somebody behind her – a kind of triangle and two."

• Missouri forward Christine Flores: "If you play in fear against her, it's game over. It's a mental preparation thing when playing Baylor because there is no player like her in the country. You have to alter your shot or drive and try to draw a foul."

● Pat Riley on Working Through Tough Times

Never demean the time you spend as a bench warmer or lowly assistant coach. If you pay attention to what you are doing, you can learn an awful lot about the way an organization behaves and that can be very useful to you later on. Use any time when you are not on center stage to strengthen your powers of perception.

Example: During my years as a player and assistant coach I learned how the Lakers operated as an organization. I knew each and every one of those players' personalities. When the opportunity to take over as head coach came, I was ready.

Keep reminding yourself that attitude is the mother of luck. Many assistant coaches believe they will never get a chance at a head job. Many head coaches are always looking over their back thinking about losing their job. You can't worry about it. You have to keep looking forward. Some long time assistants worry about developing trench stigma because they have been in a secondary position for so long. These coaches radiate fear, anxiety and defeat. Don't be one of them.

• Rick Pitino's Pre-Game Speech

Immediately before the Sweet 16 game against Michigan State, college basketball coach Rick Pitino addressed his team in the locker room. The message was simple but effective.

He asked his team to think about the many people in the audience who had never seen Louisville play basketball before: "What kind of impression will you leave those people – from the first moment when you walk out of the locker to the final whistle? Will they say, 'That team worked as hard an any I've ever seen. They maxed out every possession on both sides of the floor.' You make them say that tonight and you are 1 game from the Final 4." Louisville won and then beat Florida the next week to advance to the Final 4.

• Billy Donovan's Video Motivation

Former Florida coach Billy Donovan used the team's Elite 8 loss against Butler the previous year as motivation for the following year's tournament run. He let his team know at various points during the season that the team's lack of hustle in the closing 5 to 10 minutes cost them a chance at the Final 4.

He played the Butler tape for them over and over, trying to get it to sink in that the effort level and doing all the little things makes a huge difference come late March.

While Florida made a deep run in the NCAA tournament, they lost again late to Louisville, this time not for lack of hustle, but from cold shooting. At that stage (Elite 8), it may have been better to show some of the highlights from the team's earlier victories instead of painful reminders of the previous year's loss. Motivation is so much about timing. What can at one point in the season be very motivational can later turn into planting seeds of doubt. Tread cautiously with negative motivation.

• Bill Self on No Distractions Final 4 Preparations

In the 2008 Final 4, Kansas stayed at the Hilton on the Riverwalk. Players were not allowed to leave the hotel. They could not leave the 17th floor, except for meals on the 22nd floor and an occasional visit to the lobby. "I didn't want them downstairs or on the Riverwalk at all," Self said. "We gave them time when they could be with their families and when their families could come to the players' rooms. Other than that, I didn't want anybody around. It really didn't have the feel of a festive hotel in a large part because security had it where you couldn't get into the hotel without a room key. That might have taken away some fun for the fans, but it didn't bother us at all.

I told the players, 'If you are ever going to listen to me, please let it be this weekend. Don't try to return any text or phone calls. Don't try to trick the system. You're not smarter than anyone else. The rules apply to you.' We didn't confiscate their cell phones. Maybe I should have. But if you confiscate their cell phone and not let them out of their room, that's a long week. We wanted them to talk to family members."

How did the players respond to all the ground rules? "It was unbelievable," Self said. "It was the most mature group of kids all doing the right things that I've ever been around. You've got Kid Rock and whoever else playing outside the hotel and the wildest thing our guys did was stand out on the balcony and watch what was going on beneath them.

• Nate McMillan's Three C's of Timeouts

Former NBA basketball coach Nate McMillan's once led the league in a very unusual statistic: most improved performance after a time-out. Every coach who takes a time-out wants to get his or her team playing better.

After the first two possessions following a time out McMillan's teams held opponents to 38 percent shooting compared to 45 percent overall. On offense, they went from 44 to 46 percent shooting percentage and made baskets 10 percent more after a timeout. They also turned the ball over 12 percent less.

So what exactly did McMillan do during timeouts that help his team? Since he had a young team, he tried to stay composed on the sidelines and dial down his volume.

"The guys seem very ramped up already, so if I'm all fired up, they tend to stay too high," he said.

During timeout huddles, McMillan focuses on what he calls the three C's: "We want to be calm, we want to be clear about what we are doing and we want to be consistent."

His timeout philosophy was shaped by watching rival coach Dean

Smith during his playing days at North Carolina State. He noticed that Smith always seemed to have a surplus of timeouts at the end of games which allowed him to substitute players and disrupt the other team's rhythm.

"The way he used timeouts made me realize how important they were, especially in the late stages of a game," McMillan said. The Blazers took out the second most 4th quarter timeouts in the league. To maximize post-timeout success, McMillan believes in practicing the plays to be used after timeouts through the season. (Most NBA teams only work on post-timeout plays during training camp). To make sure the practice is paying off in games, McMillan has one of his assistants track every post-timeout possession. That's why the team led the league in post-timeout performance.

• Two Lessons from Coach K

1) Former All-American Bobby Hurley had been in a slump for four games in a row. Coach K had a sit-down one to one meeting with Hurley. Instead of giving him a lecture or a pep talk, Coach K showed him a five minute tape of Hurley reacting to his own mistakes. There on video was Hurley pouting, whining, pointing fingers and dropping his head.

When it was over Coach K said quietly, "Bobby, is that the message you want to send your teammates?" From that moment on, Hurley became one of the best point guards in the country.

2) Duke had just been blasted by 22 points in the ACC tournament championship game. Thirteen players had their heads down, not

saying a word after they boarded the bus. They were waiting for a good chewing out by their coach. "Fellas, listen to me," Krzyzewski said. "If we play like we're capable in the NCAA tournament, we will win the national championship."

With that he took his seat and didn't say another word. Never in his coaching career had he ever told a team they would win a title, but the moment was right.

"Players do their best listening after a loss."

• Wooden's 10 Practice Reminders to His Players

1) Before the official start of practice begins, work on two things: areas of weakness and free throws. Have fun, but no clowning around.

2) No cliques. No complaints. No criticizing teammates. No jealousy. Earn the respect of all.

3) Never leave the practice floor before talking to a coach.

4) When a coach blows a whistle, give him all your undivided attention and respond to the best of your ability.

5) Move quickly to get into position at changeover time for drills.

6) Make sure you keep your locker neat and orderly and take care of your equipment.

7) Record weight regularly.

8) Do things the way the coaches have taught, as correct habits are formed only through continued reps of modeling close to perfection.

9) When group activity is stopped to correct someone, all must pay close attention so you can avoid making the same mistake.

10) Poise, confidence, and self-control come from being the most prepared athlete you possibly can.

Losing is temporary and not encompassing. You must simply study it, learn from it, and try hard not to lose the same way again. Then you must have the self-control to forget about it and move on.

JOHN WOODEN

SECTION II

Competition Tested Basketball Coaching Methods

2. SWAG Propels Gators to Final 4

During a season when the Florida Gators went to the Final 4, they chose the motto **SWAG** before the season, standing for "*Strengthen When Adversity Grows.*" Coach Billy Donovan has also used visual effects to drive home his points.

Donovan asked forward Will Yeguete to grab a duffel bag sitting on the ground and throw it in his locker. Yeguete tried to pick it up with one hand, thinking he would toss it over his shoulder with ease. Donovan had the bag filled with weights, making it nearly impossible to carry with one hand.

"I picked it up with one hand and it wasn't easy," Yeguete said. "I was like, 'No, this is heavy.' He was like, 'Well, because you thought it was going to be easy but it wasn't.' "

Earlier in the season, Donovan made a picture of the entire team driving in a car. Players were looking all around, staring at signs about their rankings and their records. No one was looking ahead, where their car was getting ready to crash into a wall.

"Are we going to worry about the things around the peripheral or are we going to be focused on the road and the lane we're in right now?" Donovan asked. He wants the players to "chase greatness." More often than not, Florida players parrot Donovan's coachisms. If a player is caught looking too far ahead, he's not "living in the moment" or falling prey to "human elements." Donovan often asks his players to "embrace the process" and break down games by possession instead of worrying about longer stretches.

"It's just a reflection of what he's done with all of us this year and keeping us all focused on our goals," Florida point guard Scottie Wilbekin said.

Donovan even will use visual props from time to time in an effort to reach his players. Back in 2007, Donovan dressed as a cop in the locker room to get his team motivated at Auburn. Donovan compared winning on the road to a cop breaking up a campus party.

"I think if you can show players things, either through film or other visual means, you have a better chance of getting through to them," Donovan said.

3. Tom Crean on the Role of Assistant Coaches

Here are college basketball Coach Tom Crean's three functions that assistants should fulfill.

1. *Offset the mood of the head coach:* If the head coach is in a bad mood, you as an assistant need to be in a good mood. Assistants should not be carbon copies of head coaches.

"I love playing teams where the assistants act and teach just like the head coach because they just aren't prepared as well," Crean says.

2. *Always be accessible to players:* A head coach is often pulled in several directions through various responsibilities. An assistant must be available to players at all times. Players need that stability.

3. *Do what's needed:* As an assistant, Crean says, you are there to do whatever the head coach needs. An assistant's primary role is to make the life of a head coach easier. You must be a willing participant in this process.

"When I was learning under Ralph Willard (Western Kentucky and Pittsburgh) and Tom Izzo, my job was to make them Coach of the Year. I wanted to allow them to do what they do best, so I took care of the things they didn't want to do or didn't have time to do."

Coach Crean contends that "when assistants know their role and players are energized about their part on the team, then your program is certain to get better every day."

Along these lines, he encourages his assistants and other coaches he meets at clinics and camps, to learn as much as they can about as much as they can.

"Never stop learning from others. It doesn't have to be just in our sport. Look at military and business leaders. And, look at other sports. I bet you I have read more football books than anything else," Crean acknowledges.

According to Crean, "Your ultimate goal as a coach is not simply to win games ... it's to make players better — as athletes and as people. It starts with accountability on and off the court. When you expect the best from players, you don't have to harp on it day after day. Having to stress bringing energy and enthusiasm to the practice court each day gets old and tired. Expect it and expect the best from everyone associated with your squad."

4. Ben Howland's Defense-First Philosophy

When Ben Howland was hired to coach the UCLA men's basketball program, the players took a while to adjust to his principles. They have stuck to his defense-first philosophy, and the pay-off was a birth in a Final 4.

"We play tough defense every day in practice. You play how you practice. The way we are playing right now is how we practice every day," Howland said.

According to basketball legend Pete Newell: "UCLA can play a moderate man-to-man defense, then suddenly go to a real aggressive man-to-man. It's tough for teams to adjust to that."

The team also plays how they prepare. Howland is known as a fanatical film watcher who obsesses over opposing players' tendencies and strengths and weaknesses.

He has an unshakable belief in his system, stresses above all tough defense and limited turnovers. He has brought the team direction, structure and disciplined style of play that may have been lacking before his arrival.

According to senior Janou Rubin, "Our previous teams could play a little too loose. Coach Howland brought defense, toughness and structure. He pays attention to the smallest of details. Even though he is tough on us, we respond. "

Howland reinforces his defense-first philosophy several ways during games. If the Bruins force a turnover or block a shot or force a missed shot, he will shake his fist with glee.

Conversely, if a player misses an assignment or doesn't make a strong enough effort on defense, he will quickly turn to the bench and bark out someone else to check in the game.

Two words sum up his team's total commitment to defense: frequent subbing.

From the very start of his tenure at UCLA, players came to expect a quick hook from the game if they made a defensive lapse – regardless of how much talent that player may possess.

"Knowing what is expected of us on defense makes us play that much harder all the time. When someone else comes in for you and plays harder than you did, you realize that something isn't right and you need to step it up. The only reason we are still alive is because we believed in what coaches told us – defense will take us where we want to go," said guard Jordan Farmar.

5. Anatomy of College Basketball's Greatest Upset

Possibly the biggest upset in the history of college basketball took place December 23, 1982. Tiny Chaminade College from Honolulu, Hawaii beat Virginia, the number one team with the number one player, 77-72.

How the upset happened gives insight and hope for coaches looking to do the same today. First Virginia took Chaminade for granted. For most of the team, it was a chance to go on a Hawaiian vacation, not a business trip. It was easy to see why. They had the best team on paper (featuring center Ralph Sampson) and were ranked accordingly. What was there to fear from a tiny private NAIA school?

Coach Merv Lopes was part Phil Jackson, part Bobby Knight and part John Wooden. He said things like, "If you're small enough but good enough, you are big enough." The mental side of athletics always fascinated Coach Lopes. He started to work meditation into his practice after hearing a report of how it helped Boston Red Sox baseball teams in the mid-1970s.

On the week of the big game he guided the team through a meditation exercise that included explaining the game tactics he wanted to implement: "Swarm Sampson every time he touches the ball on defense, get the ball into the hands of the hot shooter on offense, etc."

He then used some individual "psych up" strategies for different players:

"What is the difference between you and Rick Carlisle?" he asked swingman Richard Haenisch. "Can he jump higher than you? Can he run faster than you?" Haenisch shook his head 'no' at each question.

Lopes continued: "The difference is in your brain. The game is played between the shoulders. The guy who gives 2 percent more effort is going to win. Two percent isn't that much. If Carlisle takes three steps, you take three and a half. If you keep doing that, it will make a difference."

One player balked. He asked what the hell Lopes was talking about.

It didn't phase Lopes. He asked similar questions to the entire starting lineup. Finally, he got to Tony Randolph, who had the near impossible task of guarding Sampson and giving up 10 inches in the process.

"Tony, just go out there and play ball. Show people that this is an exciting game. Just go out and have some fun."

No mention of winning the game, but they did and made history in the process.

6. Denny Crum on Lessons Working with John Wooden

"Coach Wooden's teaching was so effective because he was so well organized with his details. Everything was written on either 3 x 5 cards or notebooks. It was down to exact times. From 3:07 to 3:11 we would do X. From 3:11 to 3:17 we would do Y. Nothing was left to chance. Every single minute was accounted for.

Here is something that set Coach Wooden apart from the majority of his peers. He NEVER thought he knew everything. In spite of all his championships, he wanted to keep learning. When I first joined his staff, I brought along some of my own ideas – which he welcomed. Those he liked, he put into our practices. If they worked, fine. If not, he took them out.

He never thought his way was the only way. He continued that mentality right up to his final game. We used to have disagreements, really argue about things. People would ask him about that and he would say, "I don't want 'yes men.' If they are going to say yes to everything, I don't need them around."

When I shared an idea, he would never say, 'This is the way we've always done it and we've won a bunch of titles. I'm not changing.' Instead he was open to change and always searching for ways to improve.

In the daily coaches meetings, there was never outside interruptions. We would evaluate the previous day's practice – what worked and what needed work. What new agenda items – if any – needed to be added. There was constant adjustment and refinement.
Then we started with a minute-by-minute formatting. We would have change of pace drills, change of direction drills, defensive sliding drills, reverse pivot, etc. We would put down our plans in notebooks.

Though it all was a wide open exchange of ideas and opinions, he was tough and would critique your ideas, so you had to know your stuff to get him to change. He never did something on a whim. You had to have your reasons in place, but he would let you have your say.

Once everyone else weighed in on an idea, he made the final decision and that was it. Coach Wooden never talked about winning or losing. He would never come in before a game and say, 'This team is tied with us in the conference so we've got to step it up and win this one tonight.'

Sometimes he wouldn't even scout the other team. His philosophy was to do what was necessary to make UCLA a better team. Teach it, practice it. The details and fundamentals were his primary concern. He was completely absorbed in improvement for our team without always adjusting to what another team might do. His formula was simple: fundamentals, conditioning, play together as a team. Be great at those three and winning would take care of itself."

7. Bill Self Final 4 Pre-game Speech

Giving a pre-game speech is not an every game occurrence for Kansas' head basketball coach. Self noted after the game the speech was "made for TV" because he didn't curse once.

"I probably give speeches seven or eight times a year. I just do them when I feel our team needs it or if we're the better team and I think we're flat. I'm not very good at it," Self said.

Fire and brimstone tend to lose their potency when they are used every contest. Self used former Oklahoma football coach Barry Switzer as his example of when to give a pre-game talk: "I once heard an ex-player talk about Coach Switzer. That player told me that Switzer didn't often give a pre-game speech, but when he did the players really looked forward to them and couldn't wait to get into the locker room." He would usually save the speeches for important games.

Before the national semi-final with North Carolina, the CBS cameras would be rolling, so Self spent some time practicing his speech in the hotel room. He admitted to being more nervous about the speech than the game itself.

Here is how he addressed the team: "As coaches, we want you to know how proud we are and how happy we are for you and how much we appreciate your efforts to get to San Antonio. But getting here was tough, wasn't it? And the pressure we felt getting here wasn't deserved. It was because of that pressure that Kansas had been to three Elite Eights the last five years and hadn't gotten here yet. We felt that pressure last weekend, but we still prevailed, right? This week you guys handled it great. There's absolutely no pressure. This is the week we relax and have fun. My challenge to you tonight is for you is to have as much fun playing as I am coaching. If you do that, we're going to have a great time. I guarantee you that. We're playing a very good team, a team with great history and tradition. You know what? They are playing a very, very good team with unbelievable history and tradition. You came to Kansas to play in this game. You can't hope that good things will happen tonight. You expect them to happen and they will.

Go out and relax the best way you can. Know it's a long game and know there's going to be some anxious moments. Enjoy every second of it guys. You deserve it. But always remember, as Coach

Lombardi said, 'The most competitive men love the most competitive games.' This is one of those times. We all know how competitive you are, right? I expect there to be a big celebration in here in about 2 and ½ hours. Everybody got that?"

8. Billy Donovan on Trying to Repeat a National Championship

The Florida Gators basketball team quest to become the first team since the 1991/92 Duke Blue Devils presented a unique psychological challenge for master motivator and former head Coach Billy Donovan.

From the start, Donovan preached that five returning starters didn't mean that this team was defending anything. Just saying it wasn't enough, however, so during the Midnight Madness start to their season, Donovan allowed their 2006 championship trophy to fall from his hands and crash into pieces. The trophy was fake, but his point was made. This was a new team, a new season.

During the season, Donovan brought in an assortment of guest speakers. He invited Coach Bill Belichick of the New England Patriots, who offered the Gators a metaphor about having to start over from the bottom of a mountain they had climbed the year before.

"At the beginning of the season, I don't think we understood what he was talking about," Gators center Joakim Noah said, "but I feel like now I can really relate and understand."

I tell every guy on our roster – you can help us win a game by making just one play.

STEVE KERR

In a previous season, Donovan asked each of his players to write the name of someone who had inspired their careers on the tops of their socks, as constant reminders that there were important people in their lives who were watching them.

He tries to give his guys something to contemplate and stir their inner spirit. For example, he might tell them the story of Michael Jordan scoring 38 points in Game 5 of the 1997 NBA Finals with a 105-degree fever; or Pete Sampras winning the 1996 U.S. Open despite being so exhausted that he vomited early in the fifth set. Donovan might bring a player to his office for an individual talk or he might put together a highlight film to remind the Gators of what they are capable of doing.

Years ago, one of Donovan's teams thought it was being worked far too hard in practice. Donovan brought in a Navy SEAL to put them in their places with tales of hell week that made their practices sound like casual workouts.

Often, Donovan's message is more educational than motivational. Before the team's first practice for the NCAA tournament game in New Orleans, they visited the Ninth Ward area that has never recovered from the damage done by Hurricane Katrina.

Donovan has taken his teams to hospitals and to the remains of the World Trade Center in New York.

During a summer tour of France before their championship season, they watched "Saving Private Ryan" before visiting Normandy Beach. The basketball messages and life lessons eventually sink in.

"Sometimes, they just need the truth," Donovan said. "If I've got to come up with a technique or to trick them into it – there's got to be some internal substance to it. I also think there's a human element, where you can have a little complacency, be unmotivated or over-confident. I think there's a way to inspire them, to get them back to the truth."

John Akers www.yahoosports.com

9. The Villanova Clutch Mindset

Some athletes are overwhelmed by performance anxiety and have great difficulty closing out games or taking the last shot. Their mind becomes cluttered with 'what ifs'... "What if I miss? What if I lose the game for my team? What if the team becomes angry with me for missing the last shot?"

They become anxious and tight, which leads to poor decision making and a lack of freedom. Instead of trying to get open, they blend in the background and basically opt out of the game hoping another player takes the last shot to decide the game.

Players can change their mentality towards closing out games by applying proven mental strategies. They can definitely become the player to sink the game-ending winning shot with some practice - just like forward Kris Jenkins of the Villanova Wildcats.

He hit a three-pointer buzzer-beater to give the Wildcats a 77-74 victory over North Carolina for the NCAA tournament championship: "You know, we put a lot of work in. This team, everybody has the confidence to catch and shoot. So when Arch (Villanova guard Ryan Arcidiacono) threw me the ball, one, two step, shoot 'em up, sleep in the streets. I think every shot is going in, so that one was no different."

What gave Jenkins the confidence to hit the biggest shot of his career? Practice specificity or rehearse game situations in practice! Villanova practices last-second shots every day. When you practice under pressure situations, you acclimate to it, so during game time, you are doing what you always have done.

This type of practice doesn't eliminate anxiety, nor does it guarantee that you will make every game-ending play or shot.

Regular practice increases confidence which protects you somewhat from anxiety.

Villanova head basketball coach Jay Wright knows the value of being mentally prepared in critical situations and credits that mental preparedness for his team's ability to produce in the clutch.

According to Wright, "We do practice that. We have certain plays with less than four seconds, from four to seven seconds. Every coach has this. Zero to four, four to seven, seven to 12. We have plays. So we know what it is. We practice it every day. I didn't have to say anything in the huddle. We have a name for it, that's what we're going to do. Just put everybody in their spots."

If athletes prepare thoroughly for different game scenarios, they will approach those situations feeling like, "been there, done that" instead of being overwhelmed by fear.

Good mental preparation is all about being prepared to cope with any situation you're faced with.

Recommendation: Here is a great strategy for developing a crunch time mentality:

Write out a script for how you like to close out a tight game including: how you want the ball, the excitement of taking the last shot, a feeling of confidence with the ball in your hands, seeing the ball go through the net as time runs out and the excitement and celebration on the floor afterwards.

Take this script and act it out in practice. Make it a part of your everyday routine. You will soon see your confidence and freedom improve, as well as your mental approach to taking the "BIG" shot.

Patrick Cohn, Pd.D. www.peaksports.com

10. Betsy Blose on Building Women's Team Unity

Known as a turn around specialist when she took the head basketball job at UNC Asheville, former coach Betsy Blose, faced a new challenge – maintaining a program that had faced some setbacks the previous two years. She is the first coach to lead the team to a conference championship and NCAA birth. But after four straight winning seasons, she has seen the program take a step back. The coach is now turning student herself. She has hired a personal development 'life coach consultant' to improve her skills as a coach. Part of her new routine includes keeping a journal that she writes in every day for 30 minutes. The entries include mission and vision statements, along with day to day goals and general reflections on life away from the court. It's a daily mental break that helps her be a better coach.

When she first took over in 2002, she did some major house cleaning and posted a 3-25 record. The next year the team went 19-9 and UNCA was the most improved team in the nation – the third best turn around in D1 history.

One of the techniques she has implemented for the first time this year was a preseason team building exercise called "Vision Board." In it, she asked each player to create a poster board collage of magazine and newspaper pictures and personal photos that meant something special to each individual. Blose took the lead and shared her Vision Board first. In it, she had pictures of her six sisters, "American Idol" stars, and Tennessee basketball coach Pat Summit. The headline "flat abs" was also included. Blose's uncharacteristic request to the team to share more of a personal side was an Oprah style departure for the hard-nosed coach.

"You are sharing your values, what's important to you, so each player had to be a little bit more vulnerable than usual. You had to let people into your life in a new more personal way," Blose said. "I was amazed at how emotional the session got. But I'm now really big on these types of shared experiences that bring a group closer together."

Blose is seeking to be the best leader and team builder possible and has changed up her coaching style this year in an effort to get better results. In the past, Blose said her intensity and drive led her to hammer home tough lessons during practice. She had no tolerance for players who didn't follow team rules. She said one of her mistakes was going overboard in her criticism of team mistakes. "You get so intense sometimes, that you lose sight of what's important," she said.

There is now a renewed acknowledgement that there's more to basketball than diagrams and shootarounds. She wants to see more team spirit. In that regard, she has asked players to get their family members more involved in the program.

"Basketball is such a great vehicle for teaching life's lessons. Working with others, making sacrifices and serving the team and community are all important. The gym and film room are as much a classroom for that work as setting screens and switch defenses. Every team is different and every dynamic is different. You have to let go and learn and get better, both as players and coaches."

11. Rick Pitino on the Precious Present

Every year I start off our first practice by gathering the players around me and telling them a meaningful story. I read them a little book called the Precious Present by Spencer Johnson. It only takes about 5 minutes to tell. The story is about a little boy and an old man and the wisdom that comes with age.

"You have a great gift," the old man tells the bo

precious present and it's the best present a person can receive because anyone who receives such a gift is happy forever!"

"Wow!" the little boy said. "I hope someone gives me the precious present. Maybe I'll get it for Christmas."

The old man smiled as the little boy ran off to play. As the years passed, the boy would approach the old man and ask him again and again about the precious present. After all, the boy knew about toys. So why couldn't he figure out what the precious present was? It had to be something special, he knew, because the old man had said it would bring happiness forever.

"Is it a magical thing?" the boy asked.

"No," the old man replied.

"How about sunken treasure left by pirates?" the boy asked.

As he got older he started feeling uncomfortable asking, but he still really wanted to know what the present was.

Finally, the boy, now a young man, became annoyed. "You told me that anyone who receives such a present would be happy forever. I never got such a gift as a child!"

"I'm afraid you don't understand," the old man said.

"If you want me to be happy, why don't you just tell me what the precious present is?"

50

"And you probably want to know where to find it as well. I would like to tell you, but I have no such power. No one does. Only you have the power to make yourself happy."

The young man left, packed his bags and began a lifelong quest to find the precious present. He looked everywhere – caves, jungles, oceans. He read books, looked in the mirror and studied other people. But he never found the precious present.

Finally, after many years, when he became an old man, it finally hit him to what the precious present is. It's just that: **The Present.** Not the past and not the future, but the **precious present.**

It's not a toy. It's not a gift. It's the ability to live in the present tense. This is such an important lesson to convey to players. We become so caught up with what people say and what others think about us. We become obsessed with our failures that they consume us. We become focused on yesterday and the mistakes of the past.

Yesterday's problems are just that – yesterdays. They are a done deal. There is nothing you can do about that day except learn from your mistakes. And if it isn't the past, we are stressed about the future. We all get anxious about the future, but must learn to minimize these times. I want my players to live in the precious present. I want to live there too: to coach and live like every day is my last and not take anything for granted. It's not easy in our anxious society, but you would be amazed how simply concentrating on a task, apart from worry and regret, can be a gratifying, peaceful and positive experience.

12. Villanova Bans Cell Phones During Tournaments

The night before every game in the NCAA tournament, the players on Villanova's basketball team will hear knocks on the doors of their hotel rooms. They're being robbed.

But the thief is one of their coaches — and he wants their technology. He confiscates all their electronics and removes the Wildcats from the modern world: no laptops, no tablets and, worst of all, no cell phones.

"I feel naked without it," says freshman guard Donte DiVincenzo.

Their most unusual tactic sometimes comes as a shock to players. It often produces anxiety, and it has even inspired resistance tactics. That's what happens when you take phones away from college students.

"They're kids," said Villanova coach Jay Wright. "They don't know how to focus."

Wright has been enforcing this technology curfew for so long that he doesn't remember exactly when it started. He says his cell phone sequester may even go back to his time at Hofstra, where he was the coach until 2001, six years before the first iPhone was released.

By now, the players know what to expect. Before every road game, usually around 10 or 11 p.m., a Villanova staffer will go from hotel room to hotel room collecting all of the players' electronics.

The rush to retrieve their devices starts as soon as the players wake up — even before team breakfast.

A whole night without phones is about as long as Villanova's players can last. They scramble to scroll through a full night's worth of Snapchats, texts and Instagrams — because they know they're about to have their phones stolen again.

That happens when they enter the locker room before games. Villanova's coaches no longer have to yell "headphones!" to get them to remove their earbuds and pay attention. **No phones in the locker room means no personal music, and that means the players have to do something crazy: talk to each other.**

Villanova freshman forward Dylan Painter remembers his bewilderment the first time his phone was taken. The Wildcats were on a preseason trip to Spain over the summer when he got a knock on his hotel room door asking him to surrender his devices. He remembers thinking: "Wait, why?"

The reason is simple: There is mounting evidence that sleep is vitally important to athletes, and nobody struggles getting to bed at a reasonable hour more than young people. Electronics are a scourge to sleep because of the wavelengths of blue light that interrupt circadian rhythms and mess with our body clocks. But cell phones are especially bad: 20% of people between 19 and 29 years old are woken by an email, phone call or text message several times every week, according to a poll by the National Sleep Foundation.

That can't happen when Villanova's players aren't reachable. It also helps that the nights before games are when the phones of college basketball players blow up the most. It's when people "ask for this, ask for that," Wildcats junior Phil Booth said. Without their phones, the players are left with the televisions in their hotel rooms, and each other.

"The only thing to do," Booth said, "is fall asleep."

Other programs have experimented with this idea. But few have taken such drastic measures. Michigan State coach Tom Izzo banned phones during team meetings and bus rides in 2013. But he wasn't willing to get any more extreme. "If I took the phones away the whole time, my guys would die," Izzo said. The Spartans are now allowed to have their phones on the bus, but they stash them in a cabinet during team meetings, according to a team spokesperson.

13. The Core Tenets of Loyola Basketball

In the middle of the Loyola University basketball locker room, Aher Uguak sat quietly dressing for practice until his coach put the player on the spot.

"Shadow!" Coach Porter Moser shouted to Uguak, "What does that mean, Aher?"

Uguak stood up to demonstrate. First, he located the writing on Loyola's "*Wall of Culture*," a collection of individually painted basketball words and phrases in capital letters that serve as daily subliminal reminders, like personal Post-It notes players take pride in memorizing. *SHADOW.* "Shadow means when the offensive player is dribbling up against a main defender guarding him, and a help defender is shadowing him to make sure he doesn't get to the middle or open lane," Uguak announced, looking to Moser for approval.

Moser nodded as he elaborated, surveying the room for his next contestant. Enter junior guard Clayton Custer, who embodies everything right about Loyola basketball. The Wall of Culture are buzzwords to live by plastered all over the wall that talks.

GET OUT OF THE MUD. "After a defensive rebound, the bigs have to win the battle in the first three steps and beat the other big guys down the floor," Custer said without hesitation.

THROUGH YOU TO THE RIM. "If a guy picks up his dribble in the post, don't jump for a shot fake — he has to go through you to get to the rim," Custer said.

NEVER BE THREE IN A ROW. "You have to move to create a passing lane between me, you and the defender — don't be three in a row," Custer said.

"It's amazing the way he has gotten us all to believe in his vision for us," Custer said. "The big thing this year is the buy-in to his style of play. We're selfless."

This was the cultural impact Moser hoped for when he came up with the idea for the wall shortly after arriving at Loyola in 2011.

Four seasons on the staff of late coach Rick Majerus at St. Louis taught Moser to fixate on fundamentals. Majerus could have written a dissertation on a jump stop.

"When I got the job and was writing down all these things I wanted to do philosophically, all these details from notes when I worked for Rick, I was like, 'Let's just put it up there so they see it every day and buy in,' " Moser said. "This was a blank wall when I got here."

Now, Moser's team wins big games by doing the little things. Now, every term triggers a memory.

REACH FOR THE LIGHTS. "It's the verticality rule, when you're defending a shot, reach for the lights like Ben Richardson did and his guy missed a key layup and we won," Moser said.

NEVER QUIT ON A PLAY. "We're up two in a game with 30 seconds left and Lucas sprinted from half court and blocked a shot from behind on a wide open layup because the kid hesitated," Moser said. "We won because Lucas never quit."

The same type of perseverance carried Moser through the most difficult part of his coaching career.

Majerus' influence can be seen from the Wall of Culture to Loyola's teaching room with theater seats to the hands-on coaching style Moser copied from his mentor.

Moser doesn't worry about controlling what he can't.

"Our guys have a great mentality," Moser said. "We don't have a Missouri Valley Conference banner. Sometimes success can breed a lackadaisical mentality, like we've arrived. But we haven't. We're still chasing."

STILL CHASING. You can bet every Rambler knows what that means.

That motto helped sustain them all the way to the Final 4.

Excerpted from a Chicago Tribune article by David Haugh.

14. Rick Pitino's Five Components of Success

Here are college basketball coach Rick Pitino's thoughts on individual athlete motivation, positive confidence building, and handling competitive pressure.

I know firsthand that much of one's success in life depends on an individual's frame of mind and willingness to change for the better. If we vividly imagine success and fight off the discouragement that emerges along the way, we will have a better shot at reaching our goals.

Here are the most important steps to improve your odds of success ...

1) Set big goals, start with smaller ones ... and see yourself achieving them. To succeed at anything in life, you must be able to envision a brighter future for yourself. Whether it's losing weight or getting a promotion, you must be able to envision yourself getting what you want.

Only then can you move on to breaking down your big goals into dozens of smaller targets that can be accomplished in short periods of time. Your vision will help remind you why you're putting in such hard work or enduring such self-denial.

Example: Richie Farmer was a legendary high school basketball player in eastern Kentucky. Shortly after he came to the University of Kentucky in 1988, he and I ran into problems.

He wanted to excel, but first he had to get into better shape. One day, he complained about the rigorous weight training exercises I had set up for him. He told me that playing basketball was no longer fun and he was thinking of quitting.

Instead of comforting him, I was direct. "You're 15 pounds overweight and in terrible shape," I said. "You're being asked to lift weights and push your body, and you're telling me it's not fun. It's not supposed to be fun. The fun comes when you run out on the court in front of the greatest college basketball fans in the world."

I linked the immediate goal — getting in shape by doing intensive weight training day after day to his life-long dream. I tried to make him visualize what it would feel like to be part of a great Kentucky team.

Eventually, Farmer became a key player for the Wildcats. When he left Kentucky in 1992, his jersey was raised to the top of the school's arena.

2) See everything you do in a positive light. Negativity is the enemy of success. If you think a goal is impossible, the odds are that it will be.

Helpful: Recognize that, although you can't control the world, you can control your frame of mind. Focus on the upside of any tough situation. If you have finished half of a big assignment, you could moan about all the work that's left to do ... or you could think, "I'm halfway home, and I'm going to do such a good job that this assignment might really help my career."

Program yourself to be positive. You can get in the habit of always seeing the glass as half full.

Example: I'm much more positive now than I used to be. In my first head coaching job at Boston University, I would call timeouts at critical moments and tell my team what they had done wrong and what could go wrong on the next critical play if they didn't shape up.

Eventually, I realized I was doing a lousy job of encouraging my players. A few important losses helped convince me.

If we are fortunate to play in the NCAA tournament, I will sometimes call a timeout with less than 10 minutes left and the game is close one way or the other.

Instead of pounding on the errors we had made, I will emphasize just one thing. The players should cherish the moment they are experiencing forever. I told them that right now, at this very moment, they were doing something that every college basketball player dreams about. I told them to play as if they wanted the game to last forever. More times than not, we've advanced far.

3) Adopt the attributes of role models. One of my more recent role models is Jerry Rice, the great wide receiver for the San Francisco 49ers.

When I read about Rice's off-season workout routine, I was stunned. He is the greatest receiver in NFL history, but every day during the off-season, he puts his body through an incredible workout. I showed the Wildcats the article and said, "Look what this man does to create and maintain his physical edge. Lots of guys say they want to be the best, but they're not really willing to do the little things. Here's a guy who does all the little things and the big things."

We all learned from Rice's dedication.

4) Thrive on pressure, not stress. To keep from withering when life's challenges emerge, I find it helps to distinguish between pressure, which is healthy, and stress, which is not.

Pressure is what we put on ourselves when we set high standards for excellence and we struggle to meet or exceed those standards.

Stress, on the other hand, is negative energy that is caused by external forces when we're not focused or prepared for challenges.

If you separate the two, you're less likely to be discouraged when frustration arises or difficulties present themselves.

5) Make pressure an ally. When you feel that what you're experiencing is pressure —when you recognize that something is really important and you should do your best —remind yourself that you've worked hard to be ready for this moment, that you've done all you could do and you're now ready to give it your best shot.

15. Coaching Greatness Examples from Four Legends

Here are four coaching legends on what made them great as described by their former players.

Dean Smith on Communication During Timeouts. *By Matt Doherty.* In the 1982 championship game, I missed a foul shot that allowed Georgetown to post a go ahead score. With 30 seconds left, Coach Smith calls a timeout. Even though he was such a gifted coach, he had never won an NCAA championship and at that time was criticized as the best coach to never win one. But his demeanor in that high pressure situation was amazing. He talked to us in such a calm manner that it gave us the confidence to go out and execute. In those situations, where the players were visibly anxious, he had a calming influence on us. I've been around other coaches who did just the opposite. They took a tense situation and added more pressure, making players even more nervous.

With Coach Smith, he always made you feel like, "Hey, isn't this fun? We're right where we want to be." He always had a look in his eye that made you feel confident. During that timeout, he pulled me aside and said, "If you are open, knock it down." He made everyone feel like that if they were open, they could make the shot. Fortunately, it was Michael Jordan who hit the game winner with 17 seconds left.

Red Auerbach on Player/Coach Communication. *By Tommy Heinsohn.* What Red did better than anyone else is to get people committed to excellence. He even coined a phrase for it – Celtic Pride.

Here is an example of how he instilled that commitment to excellence. We were down 10 points with around two minutes left in a game. We all gathered round in the team huddle and knew he had five plays immediately ready to give us right at his disposal to help us win the game. Instead, he looks around and says, "Has anyone got anything?" By that, he wanted to know what you thought you could do to help win the game. It was a simple, but great technique that gave us pride of authorship to anyone who came up with a good idea. This happened many times during my career. Red would ask the question and get feedback. Then he would say, "Ok, we will use your's first, your's second, and your's third."

Red wanted us engaged in the thinking part of the game – right from training camp. At the first practice, he would say, "Guys, I'm thinking about adding this play this season. He would diagram and demonstrate the play to us. Then he would solicit our thoughts and ideas on how effective it would be. (One caveat: rookies were not allowed to give feedback. That was something earned after being with the team at least a year.) It's no coincidence that so many former Celtic players eventually became head coaches.

John Wooden on Execution. *By Gail Goodrich.* When I think of Coach Wooden, the first word that comes to mind is execution. We never worried about the opponent – only about how we were going to play. Coach never even had us watch film of other teams. During our 1964 title game against Duke, that may have been a good thing. During warm-ups, we certainly noticed they had a couple of 6'10" players, where our tallest starter was 6'5". Coach didn't sound the least bit worried as he came into the locker room to give his pre-game speech. "Look," he said. "We got here playing a certain way. We'll press and make this a full, 94 foot game. They're bigger, but we're quicker. We'll get off the boards and run. If we've got the break take it. If not, we'll get into our offensive set quickly." Then he paused a minute and asked us the question: "Who remembers who came in second place last year?" No one raised his hand. Then he looked at us one by one in the eye and finally said, "No one remembers who finished second last year. Now get out there and play your best."

Pat Summitt on Recruiting. *By Michelle Snow.* During recruiting, I called Coach Summitt and told her I wasn't going to come to Tennessee. She was still in practice and I could tell her patience was short. She simply said, "Ok, I'll see you tomorrow." I was thinking, yeah right, is she going to fly down to Pensacola, Florida and convince me to come to Tennessee?

Sure enough, the next day she came to visit me in person. She told me, "You said you wanted to be one of the best players in the country. To be one of the best, you've got to play against the best. We have one of the top rosters in the country." Then she showed me a piece of paper that she had folded in half. On one side, she wrote

Tennessee (UT) and on the other side, she wrote the name of the other school I was about to commit to. She wrote the words Championships, which listed 6 under UT and 1 under the other school. On the next line she wrote Olympians and number 8 next to UT and 0 for the other school. Next she wrote players in the WNBA and the advantage for UT was 6 to 2. There were more numbers favoring UT listed down the page.

While she read, she wasn't really looking at me – it felt like she was burning a hole through my head. As much as I wanted to go to the other school, I knew that everything she was telling me was right. I committed to UT a few days later.

As a coach, if you can get your players to play hard and together on defense, they will automatically be unselfish on the offensive end.

LARRY BROWN

SECTION III

Practice Techniques that Get Results

(Includes Special Section on Improved Free Throw Shooting)

16. Seven Practice Planning Questions

Sometimes teams get so busy going through the repetitive motions of practice drills that they get stuck and fail to improve.

You can help them reduce inefficiencies and make the best use of practice time by asking yourself (and sometimes the team) the following questions:

1) How can I maximize our practice time and schedule to get the absolute maximum benefit?

2) Are we doing our tasks or drills in the best order?

3) Do we spend too much down time waiting between drills or during drills that could be changed?

4) Do we anticipate problems before they arise and have a plan to handle them?

5) Does everyone understand our tasks and timelines?

6) Is there any portion of practice that can be changed or dropped at a certain point in the season without sacrificing performance? (For example, less running later in the season when the team may be worn down).

7) Is the equipment we have helping us maximize our players' abilities or do we need to change or upgrade it?

17. Use Contracts to Improve Practice Commitment

To keep the desire to train and drill high during the long off season you can use a simple method proven effective for treating the over-weight and rehabilitating heart patients. It's called contracting.

Recommendation: Behavior contracting is a sure way to avoid staleness and can be readily applied to enhance training and practice compliance. There are five steps involved:

1. *Define the problem.* Specify in behavioral terms what the athlete is not doing. For example, a basketball player is not spending the extra time necessary to improve free throw percentage. 2. *Define the goal.* Get the player to make the commitment to shoot free throws for 15 minutes after practice. 3. *Define control strategies.* Provide specific cues, which will help remind the player to execute the desired play. Examples include setting up a specific time for shooting free throws, putting a poster of Michael Jordan on their locker for inspiration, or having a competition with another player. 4. *Define the contract.* Put the goals, cues, rewards and punishments in writing. Prior to the season, you must set up the specific rewards and punishments for compliance or non-compliance to the program. Both the player and coach must actually sign the contract. 5. *Monitor and evaluate the program and implement the proper rewards or punishments.*

P.S. The process will only be effective if the athlete understands what the program's goals are and what the rewards or consequences will be.

Thomas Collingwood, Ph.D.

18. Push Superior Players with Tougher Drills

One of the problems associated with coaching superior athletes is providing competitive challenges for them in daily practice, especially when one athlete is far superior to his or her teammates. Without sufficient challenges, such athletes may develop a half-hearted work ethic that inhibits their progress. The solution to this problem lies in creating competitive situations in which the athlete's skills are taxed beyond what he or she might normally expect. If your superstar isn't sufficiently challenged in your drills and scrimmages, perhaps a permanent double-team can increase the resistance enough to provide a suitable challenge.

With one outstanding player, you can have him or her play one-on-two in your competitive drills. With two superior players at the same position, you can pit them one-on-one against each other or have them go two-on-three against their teammates.

If there is a noticeable drop off in quality beyond your first string, add one or more extra players to the other team in scrimmages. The more pronounced the disparity, the more advantages you may need to equalize the teams.

In practicing half court defense — zone or man-to-man — try stationing a sixth offensive player in the middle of the lane (and ignore the three-second rule, of course). In full court pressing defensive drills, try putting at least six players on offense. You can go five on three because you will seldom have the luxury of coaching ten quality players at a time. Tell the starters, "That's the price you have to pay for being a starter. If you're a starter, you work harder."

19. Vary Practice Drills to Keep Things Fresh

You incorporate drills and activities to reinforce development of your athletes' physical skills and strategic plans.

Just as repetition leads to execution for physical and team skills, mental skills are best learned through actual practice and game-like settings. Mental skills such as decision making, recognizing play patterns, focusing attention, etc. are best learned and reinforced while physically performing.

Examples: *A track coach has runners rotate interval starting and finishing positions around the track so they won't adopt a mental set, pushing during one stretch but coasting during another. Changing starting and finishing positions forces runners to mentally concentrate on their pace at every position around the track.*

A volleyball coach changes how points are scored during scrimmages. Players can lose form, not run plays properly and still score points, but this defeats the purpose of scrimmaging. Rather, award points for passing accurately, moving without the ball, and calling out. The team that plays the best scores the most points. This reward structure reinforces mental decisions that lead to more effective play in actual games.

A basketball coach has players practice grabbing rebounds underneath the basket and shooting layups with each hand. However, a mental error is dropping the ball below the shoulders where it could be stolen. Positioning another player in front of the rebounder ready to swat at the ball if dropped below the shoulders is great way to reinforce the mental decision to keep the ball away from other players.

Recommendation: Here are steps to help you modify drills and activities to incorporate mental practice. First, think of the mental skills needed for your sport or demands of your sport that affect mental processes. Second, determine how the practice drills and activities you already use incorporate mental skills. If they do, exaggerate the emphasis on mental skills. If they don't, modify the drills to include mental reinforcement. Third, experiment! Be bold in trying new activities, altering traditional scoring schemes, rewarding play rather than outcome. Some will work, some will not. In any case, you will be practicing mental skills necessary for coaching.

Steve Houseworth, Ph.D.

20. Structure Practice to Meet Athlete Motives

Does it seem your athletes are just "going through the motions" in practice? Structuring your practice sessions to satisfy the motives of your athletes can increase motivation and intensity. The first step is to find out why your athletes compete. Asking them to write reasons down on a preseason questionnaire can do this. Once you understand their motives, you can select coaching strategies to optimize motivation.

Four major categories of motives are most common among athletes: competence, fitness, fun, and social. Competence motives include such reasons as desiring to achieve personal goals, improve skills, and wanting to win. Fitness motives include getting in shape, and increasing strength and endurance. Fun involves the action, challenge, and excitement of competition.

Athletes involved for social reasons may enjoy the teamwork and team spirit involved in sport. Based on their reasons for team membership, you can structure the athletic environment to meet these reasons, or motives for participation. By doing so, you help enhance motivation to ensure maximal effort and persistence.

Recommendation: Here are suggestions for satisfying the four motives for athlete participation. *Competence motives:* 1. Provide informational feedback, i.e. tell the athlete what to do, instead of what not to do. 2. Give effective skill demonstrations. Provide a "show and tell" model, and use effective cue phrases to direct attention. 3. Provide optimal challenges for all athletes. Establish individual performance goals to encourage maximal effort.

Fitness Motives: 1. Use practice time effectively. Plan to keep all athletes actively involved in all phases of practice. 2. Select a good variety of activities and drills. Be sure to provide activities which stress different parts of the body.

Fun Motives: 1. Provide for change of pace drills and practices. Allow the team to select a drill or occasionally run a "captain's practice." 2. Stage event simulations. Bring fans in to watch practice on some days. 3. Include some activities in practice "just for fun." These activities can still work on related skill or conditioning elements.

Social motives: 1. Organize team gatherings. Get to know your athletes outside of the sport setting and allow them time to learn about each other. 2. Conduct task-oriented drills which allow for interdependent play and maximize team spirit. 3. Emphasize team goals and affirmations. Be sure to provide both outcome and performance oriented team goals and select affirmations which focus on the strengths of the team.

21. Pete Newell's Tactic to Change Practice Intensity

Former college basketball coach Pete Newell had a great method of keeping his players on their toes during practice. This comfort zone is dangerous because it creates an almost imperceptible lowering of practice intensity, focus, and energy, which leads to reduced effort, more mistakes and overall drops in performance.

Normally an upbeat coach in the Dick Vitale mode, once Newell spotted a minor miscue, suddenly his temperament changed. He would blow off steam like lightning and thunder. Soon the emotional squall would pass and Coach Newell would lighten up and use humor as practiced resumed. But it was evident to his players that they were dialed in to his demeanor, emotions and attitude. He was the focal point the players responded to.

Of course, the little "issue" that set him off, maybe a pass wasn't crisp or player out of position for a rebound – was often an excuse to fix the larger concern, which was usually the lack of intensity, energy and attention level of his players.

Players were kept on their toes because Pete Newell was somewhat unpredictable. His players knew that toughness lurked within and that he was willing and able to bring it forth when necessary.

Here's the key take-away for team leaders and coaches. Effective leaders understand that if you are *predictably* difficult, *predictably* easygoing, others become *predictably* comfortable. In a highly competitive environment, feeling comfortable is first cousin to being complacent.

When legendary college and professional football Coach Bill Walsh would sense from time to time that the team or staff was getting too comfortable, he would exercise what acting skills he could muster.

This could be letting his emotions suddenly boil over, throw down his clipboard, or publicly chew out an assistant coach (they understood that the ultimate message was for the players). Taking a cue from Coach Newell, Walsh would say things during a poor practice like, "I can't take this anymore. We've got to pick up the effort or I'm going to make changes because *this* has to stop."

The players didn't have to know what *"this"* Walsh was referring to. The point was to bring them out of their comfort zone. Practice is a time when complacency and going through the motions can creep in and teams need to jolt them back into a businesslike attitude.

Walsh and Newell were both careful not to let these outbursts move into personal attacks on individual players.

22. Eight Rules for More Effective Communication

In his book *Words that Work,* author Frank Luntz talks about effective political communication with the bottom line being how to get your message across in the most direct methods. He lists several rules for effective language that coaches can gain insight from as well.

The rules of language are especially important given the sheer amount of communication each person has to contend with. We step out of our houses into a nonstop sensory assault: advertising and entertainment, song lyrics, commercial jingles, abbreviated emails, text messages and fast conversations. From inside our homes comes more noise in the form of televisions, computers and iPods. How do you get your communication to rise above all this chatter?

Here are eight of Luntz's rules for successful communication.

Rule 1. Simplicity. Use small words. Avoid words that might make someone reach for the dictionary.

Rule 2. Brevity. Use short sentences. Be as brief as you can when describing what you want to communicate. Never use a sentence when a phrase will do.

Rule 3. Credibility is as important as philosophy. People have to believe it to buy it. If your words lack sincerity or if they contradict accepted facts, circumstances or perceptions, they will lack impact.

Rule 4. Repetition and consistency matter. One that every coach knows but it bears repeating. Repetition of message is critical. Hammering home key points over and over is important. Good language is like the energizer bunny. It keeps going and going.

Rule 5. Sound and texture matter. The sounds and texture of language should be just as memorable as the words themselves. A string of words that have the same first letter or sound is more memorable than a random collection of sounds.

Rule 6. Speak with team aspirations in mind. You want to personalize the message to trigger an emotional connection or response that the whole team can relate to.

Rule 7. Paint a word picture. When advertisers come up with slogans that have a lasting impact like "Must See TV" (NBC) or "Melts in Your Mouth, not in Your Hands" (M & Ms), the slogans paint a mental picture that the audience can see and almost feel.

Rule 8. Ask a question. "Got Milk?" may be one of the most memorable print advertising campaigns of the past decade. A statement, when put in the form of a rhetorical question can have a much greater impact than a plain assertion.

23. Player Post-Game Self Evaluations Improve Performance

Coaches and athletes must deal with the fact all games end with a team's performance falling (more or less) into one of the following categories: 1) *Won and played well.* 2) *Won but played poorly.* 3)

Lost and played well. 4) *Lost and played poorly.* Given the above four conditions, is there a constructive method when debriefing a team so players will utilize the just-ended contest as a learning experience?

Athletes will be prone to openly demonstrate anger and disappointment following a game when their team plays poorly. These exaggerated postmortems are non-constructive, expressed with negative emotion and mostly inaccurate. They distort the coach and players' perceptions of what actually took place on the court or field. Fueled by negative emotion, the coach may also inaccurately attribute the team's poor play or loss to factors, after careful analysis, had a minimal impact on the team's performance.

Immediately following a game, especially after a poor team performance, coaches should address psychological needs, e.g. leaving alone those who prefer to be left alone, reassuring those who need confidence boosted, and ensuring no one gets "too down" or sullen. Denigrating personal remarks made to specific team members add to the inaccurate self-assessment of factors responsible for a poor performance. Even more important, it leads players to attribute their poor performance to factors far removed from the "reality of the situation."

In setting up an effective post-game debriefing program, coaches usually have two common objectives across all sports: 1. Improve individual performance. 2. Utilize the just completed game as a tool to prepare for the next contest.

Recommendation: Have players fill out an evaluation form a few hours following a game to rate how they performed. You can tailor this form to criteria of your choosing. A meeting can be held the following day to discuss the player's performance with the coach. At this meeting the coach can modify individual performance attributions and interact with the players in a positive and rational manner as sufficient time has elapsed to be objective.

For example, if the player is inaccurately self-critical, by utilizing the checklist *coaches can objectively evaluate performance and place the negative aspects in proper context.* Video review can be used here for supporting the positive. The coach can also give the team a written analysis, which stresses positive execution, while constructively stating areas that need to be improved.

The next day's meeting, with one-to-one consultation, video review, and written analysis by both coaches and athletes will be 100% more effective than any post-game session immediately following a contest.

24. John Wooden's Eight Keys to Run a Great Practice

Former UCLA basketball coach John Wooden was a master at organizing practices for maximum production. Here are his eight tips to create a great practice environment. Implement these and watch athletic motivation and engagement soar.

1. *Fundamentals before creativity:* Coach Wooden believes the teaching of fundamentals, until they are all executed quickly, properly, and without conscious thought, is prerequisite to playing the

Prepare for every game as if you just lost the last one.

LON KRUGER

game. Drills must be created so that all of the fundamentals are taught to the criterion that players execute them automatically.

In Wooden's words: "Drilling created a foundation on which individual initiative and imagination can flourish."

2. *Use variety.* Although the general skeleton of practice lessons were the same, there were lots of surprises that kept things interesting and fun. Coach Wooden "would devise new [drills] to prevent monotony, although there would be some drills we must do every single day."

3. *Teaching new material.* When creating the daily lesson plan, Coach Wooden was careful to install new material in the first half of practice, not the second. There were two reasons for this: Our minds were fresh and not yet worn down by two hours of high-intensity activities, and he could devise activities during the second half of practice for the application of new material.

4. *Quick transitions.* During Wooden's practice sessions, one witnessed lightning-quick transitions from activity to activity. Players sprinted to the next area and took pride in being the first to begin. Transitions were as intense as the activities. No time was wasted. With a little ingenuity, creativity, and organization, classrooms can be morphed from inefficient operations to efficient systems.

5. *Increasing complexity.* Drills evolved from simple to extremely complex and demanding. Every movement, every action was carefully thought out and planned.

6. *Conditioning.* Coach Wooden's philosophy is for players and students to improve a little every day and make perfection the goal. His method for improving conditioning included one painful demand — each player, when reaching the point of exhaustion, was to push himself beyond. When this is done every day, top conditioning will be attained over time.

7. *End on a positive note.* Coach Wooden always had something interesting, challenging, or fun planned for the last five minutes.

8. *End on time and avoid altering a plan during the lesson.* Once the practice started, Coach Wooden never changed it, even though he may have noticed an existing drill that needed more time or thought of a new one he should have included. The proper place for new ideas and improvements was on the back of the 3 x 5 index card, which he made notations on.

He strongly believed in ending practices on time; otherwise players might hold back, anticipating the need for energy reserves if the practice was extended. Because athletes knew the practice would stop promptly at 5:29 p.m. without exception, he felt he could maintain the intensity level throughout the session and we would be willing to extend ourselves.

25. 12 Question Practice Organization Checklist

Many coaches frequently complain that they do not have sufficient time to accomplish all the things they need in order to make practice successful. Good organization and planning can often times enhance the chances of meaningful practices.

Coach John Wooden once stated that he could go back twenty four years and tell anyone what he did at any given time on any given practice day. Regardless of the level of coaching that you are involved with, good planning and organization can usually improve your practice.

Most coaches are concerned with the loss and misuse of practice time. However, it is generally agreed upon that most practice periods can be improved with the implementation of a written plan. Most coaches also generally agree that the single most important factor in improving athletic performance is practice.

As coaches, don't we owe the players a practice plan that can improve good practice habits? If players see evidence that their coaches work diligently to prepare for an effective practice they may reciprocate by better participation. There does appear to be a significant relationship between success in games and practice organization and planning.

After guidelines have been established, the actual practice organization must take place. Practice organization should be divided into four parts. The first of these involves establishing monthly practice plans. A monthly practice schedule can be very effective for setting short-term goals for the players as well as for the coaching staff. The second part of effective practice organization is setting up a daily plan. Time periods for each phase of the game, goals for the day, and actual game skills to be practiced are three crucial elements for daily planning.

The third part of effective practice organization is the season coverage chart. This aspect may include drills, offenses, defenses, long and short-term goals and how much time will be devoted to particular offenses and defenses. The final part of effective practice organization is evaluation. Each practice should be evaluated as a basic for future practice plans. Evaluation of practice organization must be a continuous thing.

Some of these 12 rules for practice efficiency may seem like common sense, but you would be surprised that at least some of them are often overlooked.

Evaluation Checklist For Practice Organization

You can use the following criteria (always, most of the time, sometimes, never) to answer the following 12 questions. Your answers will speak volumes on whether your team is up to speed for running an organized practice.

1. Is the practice schedule for the day displayed on the team bulletin board?

2. Do the players arrive on time for practice?

3. Does the coach have a file of previous practices?

4. Does the coach have a written practice plan?

5. Does the coach frequently refer back to past practice plans?

6. Do the plans list specific time limits for each activity?

7. Does the coach have specific duties planned for each activity?

8. Do the players know what is expected of them?

9. Do the members of the coaching staff have clear cut responsibilities?

10. Does the coach have different plans for the three parts of the season?

11. Do the players gain or lose stamina and endurance during practice?

12. Do the players run drills directly related to game situations?

26. Coach Carolyn Savoy on Preparing a Team for Playoffs

Canadian women's basketball coach Carolyn Savoy authored the book 'Art of Coaching.' Here is an excerpt on preparing a team for the playoffs.

Every coach wants to know how to get his or her team to peak at playoff time. Successful coaches I interviewed said there was no magic formula for getting a team ready for the playoffs, however they did offer the following advice:

Recommendation: * Keep your team fresh. Make your practice times shorter toward the end of the season. For example, you can start down about 4-6 weeks before the end of a six-month university season, or during the last three weeks of a high school campaign. Keep the intensity level high and do not slack off on conditioning — just do everything for a little less time. Your players' bodies need the rest at the end of a long season.

* Cut down on any extra conditioning work (i.e., weight training, plyometrics, distance running, cardiovascular training on treadmill machines) outside of practices. If you require extra training during the season, start to cut down during the last few weeks. The exact amount of the reduction will depend on your game schedule. Ask a strength and conditioning expert for advice in this area.

* Monitor the amount of water that your players consume. Make sure that they always drink water during practices. As a general rule, tell the players to drink one liter of water one hour before practice, one liter of water during practice, and one liter of water after practice. Players should actually drink this throughout the entire year.

* Make sure to emphasize to the players that they need to be well rested. They have worked hard all season and have exerted a great deal of energy. Don't push them too hard late in the year.

* If a player is injured or ill, give him or her time off from practice to rest. You want everyone to be healthy and rested for the playoffs. Missing a practice in order to get a player healthy is a worthwhile investment. Unless a player has a contagious illness, they can still come to practice and support the team.

* When it's late in the season, give your team a day off so that they can do other things. This will reenergize your players — both mentally and physically.

* Show your players some video highlights from their season. Praise them for the things that they've been doing well.

* Show them some film of a former team winning the championship. It does not matter how long ago it was — the players will still get excited when they see the players celebrating a victory for the program. If some of your current players were on that championship team, the video will serve as a great reminder about how they felt at the time.

* Talk about having fun in the playoffs. Tell your players that the crowd will be excited; and that there will be lots of positive energy in the air — from each other, the coaching staff, their families, the students, and the fans.

* Ask your players: "What would you be willing to do to win a championship for your best friend on the team? What would you be willing to sacrifice?' This process creates positive energy for the players. It gets your players to focus on the common goal and teaches them life lessons about sacrifice, loyalty and commitment."— Coach Stephen Stewart, winner of six provincial women's basketball championships as the Head Coach at Queen Elizabeth High School, Halifax, Nova Scotia, Canada.

* At playoff time, you may have to calm down your players. You do not have to remind them about the importance of the games —

they know that already! Instead, tell them that this one game is not the end of the world, but simply another step in the process of building this team and developing themselves as players.

* If you are going to play an opponent that you have beaten several times, then overconfidence is always a danger. If your players seem complacent, wake them up by reminding them that this could be the last game of the season. Do not take the outcome for granted!

* If you have set high standards and demanded a lot from your team, remind them how much they've improved. Tell them that they will beat this opponent because they are superior.

* Late in the season, if a player does something that irritates you (and I'm not talking about breaking a rule or violating a fundamental team principle) — simply look the other way.

* Tell your players that they are well prepared: "We are fit, we are strong, and our skills are well honed. You've done all the hard work. Now all we have to do is play the game."

* Tell your players to focus on what they can control. Focus on our own team's play.

* Run time-and-score situations (e.g., "45 seconds to go, and we're down by one point") during the last month of practice. Remind your players that if they never give up and continue to work hard as a team, it is always possible to come from behind for a win. At the same time, remind them that they should never get too excited about what might happen (e.g., thinking that they are about to win

the game). Stay in the present. Don't start celebrating too early and lose the game.

Signs that your team may be ready:

* The team seems closer. They are less social with their opponents.

* You may see an occasional temper flare-up in practice.

* The players are excited to play and to practice.

* Your players feel relaxed because they know they're well prepared.

Signs that your team may not be ready:

* Players start trying to do things that they do not normally try to do.

* Players seem complacent. They think the championship is "in the bag" because they have already beaten all the teams.

BONUS PRACTICE SESSION: IMPROVING FREE THROWS

27. UCONN Free Throw Training

NCAA Men's champion basketball team UCONN used a special training program to get their team out of a free throw shooting slump. There was a video of former NBA star Steve Nash shooting as many free throws as he could in a one-minute segment. The premise ran counter to conventional coaching wisdom.

Rather than slowly and deliberately shooting from the line, the "Nash Drill" required players to approach free throw shooting like a kid playing a "Pop a Shot" game at Chuck E Cheese.

They started to work the drill into their training three seasons ago. Mechanically, coaches look for players to slow down motion to keep the shooting mechanics as streamlined as possible.

"If you can get rid of all the extra motion in the shot, your rhythm and your timing becomes that much better," said asst. coach Glen Miller.

Here is how the drill works: Players are paired off with one player rebounding the ball and passing to the person shooting at the line. Players usually toss in 22-24 shots in a minute. UCONN requires players to hit at least 17 out of 22 or be forced to run extra laps.

28. Wooden's Free Throw Analysis

Former player Lynn Shackleford recalled how Coach Wooden helped his free throw percentage: "One day Coach asked me to stay after practice. He told me, 'If you were standing at the free throw line and took a jump shot, you would expect to make every shot, right?' I replied, 'yea.'

He said, 'I think you are spending too much time bouncing the ball and deep breathing and all of that.' He then said he would rebound for me as I practiced. He told me, 'Just take two dribbles and shoot the ball. Don't think about it.'

So I took his advice for about 7 shots. He asked me to continue doing exactly what I was doing. I went from 75 to 90 percent with that small change. I thought to myself later, 'How did he know what I needed to do?' He made a dramatic impact in only 60 to 90 seconds of coaching."

Wooden knew a lot about the physics of motion. He knew that when you accelerate your motion, the better and straighter you're going to be. He was an uncomplicated coach. He didn't want us over thinking. He sensed I was thinking too much at the free throw line and he just wanted me to shoot it.

29. Mark Price on 13 Steps to Improve Free Throw Percentage

Mark Price retired as the NBA's all time leader in free throw percentage. Here is his success formula.

1. Find the nail. (There's a nail that marks the exact center of the foul line)

2. Center yourself so your head is directly above the nail.

3. Look at the rim. Determine if it is tilting to the left or the right. Adjust accordingly.

4. Spread your legs until your body is in its most stable position, usually with your feet about shoulder-width apart. If you're right-handed, put your left toe several inches behind the line. Do the reverse if you're left-handed.

5. Bounce the ball several times to get the feel of it.

6. Spin the ball in your hands. Grab it with the seams parallel to the floor. Don't place any part of either hand on the needle hole. No part of your palm should touch the ball.

7. Concentrate on a specific spot on the rim. (For most players it's the back center of the rim; for Price, the front center.)

8. Bend your knees and raise the ball to your head in one fluid motion. As you do this, start standing on your toes.

9. Draw the upper part of your shooting arm back so that you create an L with the lower part of the arm. The elbow of your shooting arm should be tucked in and directly below the hand. Cock your wrist at about a 60-degree angle.

10. In one fluid motion remove your guide hand from the ball and flick the wrist toward the rim. The last fingers to remain in contact with the ball should be your index and middle fingers.

11. Follow through so that your fingers point toward the rim.

12. When shooting two, step away from the foul line after your first shot, so that a teammate **will not shake or slap your hand**.

The encouragement is distracting.

13. Take 500 free throws a day in practice in the off-season and 100 a day in season. Keep track of how you're doing with a log.

30. Bobby Knight on Free Throws and Timeouts

In the book, "The Power of Negative Thinking," former college basketball legend Bobby Knight shared his thoughts on free throws and timeouts.

On Free Throw Shooting: In practice my teams shot them as most teams do – as an end to practice. But I'd do things like pull one player out in front of all the others and say, "All right Quinn, you've got a one and one. Make them both or everyone has to run five sprints." That's not a tremendous penalty but it puts a little pressure on because teammates really get on the player who misses.

More commonly, in a hard practice, I had my teams shoot free throws when I thought a rest break was needed. After we had gone hard for 20 minutes and shown good execution, I'd stop things by yelling, "Free throws!." My players knew this communicated that I was happy with what I had just seen.

Our procedure at those breaks was that groups of two would go to the various baskets around the practice court and each player would shoot two free throws each. Then they would rotate to a different basket. I always felt this accomplished several things: a needed break and a shot of confidence because something had just been done well by the team. Plus they were practicing free throws when they were tired, which is exactly what would happen late in a game.

On Timeouts: Once our players were trained to think, there was consistent indication of my trust in them. During games, I usually left them on their own to play through down periods without calling a timeout. Sometimes my intent was more of a teaching step. As the season went along, I wanted our players – individually and as a team – to have developed the ability to think and work their way through tough stretches of play.

There was one exception to my general theory of not rushing to take a timeout and that was tournament play. The single loss elimination event is final. I always tried to keep all game preparation as normal as possible in tournaments, but if things started slipping, then a quicker timeout made sense. In general, however, my theory was that if you made your ideas clear in practice, then you didn't need a timeout to reinforce them. Even more important – don't try to make a brilliant change when things are going well.

31. The Best Mental Approach to Free Throws

Note: The following chapter is based on an interview with a sport psychologist who had a consulting relationship with a Women's Division 1 basketball team. The team and consulting psychologist are unnamed because of privacy concerns.

The consulting sport psychologist (CSP) had known the head coach for many years prior to working together. It was decided by the head coach that the CSP would work with the coaching staff, the team and individual athletes once every two weeks. This chapter will address some of the intervention strategies used to help the team with their free throw shooting that were the most successful.

What techniques did you introduce to help the team improve their poor free throw percentage?

We worked with each player on their preshot routine. The goal was to get them to their ideal performance state.

The two main components of the preshot routine are appropriate arousal level and appropriate focus of attention.

First, they learned to monitor their level of arousal. Most of the student athletes needed to be more relaxed when shooting a free throw than they are during the game. To help themselves relax, some players would take a couple of deep breaths. Others would shake their arms and/or legs and others stretched a little bit.

To help acquire the proper focus, some athletes would visualize making the shot, others would verbalize cues to themselves such as "good follow through," or "nice arc." Others would verbalize positive results such as "swish" or "through the hoop."

After the athletes had developed these two components, they developed specific, individual routines they would use at the line. I stressed how important it was to be consistent and once you have a set routine, do not deviate from it.

Examples: A few would shake their arms out. Some would visualize making the shot right before they would shoot. Others didn't like to visualize and I never made anyone do something they weren't comfortable with.

One player would place one foot in front of them and wiggle it and then another, then bounce the ball three times, then spin it in her hand, see the ball go through the hoop, then shoot her free throw.

Another athlete would step to the line, wipe her hand on her left shoe, then on her right shoe, shake her legs out, dribble the ball five times, say "swish" to herself, then shoot.

Were there any drills used to help with free throw shooting?

The coaching staff asked the student-athletes to visualize various scenarios while they were practicing.

For example, a coach would say, "We are down by one with four seconds left." The whole practice would stop. An athlete would stand at the line with her teammates and coaches watching. This helped introduce a "real life" pressure situation into practice.

Another drill used toward the end of practice would be to stop the action and tell one player to go to the line. The coach would say, "Make three free throws in a row and practice is over."

Failing to prepare is preparing to fail.

JOHN WOODEN

SECTION IV

Interviews and Profiles of Coaching Legends

32. Bob McKillop on Motivation and Recovering from Failure

Long time Davidson basketball coach Bob McKillop has always been a creative motivator —sometimes old school, sometimes corny, sometimes philosophical.

A pair of plastic sunglasses. A matted tennis ball. Loose links of a chain. These are all part of the messages and teaching lessons that come from the junk drawer in his office. The plastic glasses? McKillop puts them on when a player misses an open man in practice. The tennis ball? One Davidson team bounced it around campus — a symbol of "bouncing back" after a couple of losses. The chain links? Players on another Wildcats' team brought them to games — one link per player — then put them together in the locker room before tip-off.

There are three words he tells every player, every year to focus on. Trust. Commitment. Caring. The words would mean little, he says, if you're not 'living it.'

When McKillop talks about caring, he boils it down to the essentials of basketball, like how helping a teammate helps everybody, even if it's as small as setting a screen for a teammate. McKillop calls it "making an investment."

McKillop is a man so devoted to detail, to following through, that he calls former players on their birthdays, and once learned Italian for an overseas basketball clinic.

Says his son, Matt: "There's rarely a time you see him without a piece of paper in his hand, writing things down. He wants to gain from his experiences."

It is, the coach says, what he's always looked for in recruits. Not only someone who can handle the rigors of Davidson — and its sometimes harsh basketball coach — but someone who is unsatisfied, no matter what success he's found. And failure? Yes, that's a part of Davidson, too.

Three years ago, one of McKillop's best teams lost the Southern Conference tournament and an NCAA bid after finishing the conference season undefeated. McKillop sent his devastated players encouraging emails and called them into his office. "It was so easy for them to have a pity party," he says. "I challenged them to find out what kind of men they were."

Says assistant coach Matt Matheny: "He does talk about trust. He says it to our guys whether it's playing or practice or a team meeting at his house. It's important on the court, but it carries though to life."

Excerpted from the Charlotte Observer newspaper. www.charlotte.com

33. Buzz Williams on Connecting with Players

College basketball coach Buzz Williams is a big time reader who keeps his office meticulously organized. Included are coaching autobiographies, *New York Times* business leadership best sellers and his own detailed journal with color coded entries.

His office is a tidy sanctuary. Papers are carefully stacked on Williams' desk; even the remote for his plasma television must be placed just right. Williams admits he has obsessive-compulsive habits. "Those papers have to be perfectly in order," he says. "If somebody comes in my office and changes things, it flips me out."

Williams keeps detailed notes on all the books he reads, conversations he has with his players' parents, and input from assistants. Williams keeps some of his most recent notes folded and clipped together in his pocket. His journal is a mixture of play charts, observations and reflections – all printed in upper-case letters. The remarks are made in different ink colors – his own personalized color coded scheme.

Williams encourages players to read coaching books – even different sports other than basketball. Football coaches Tony Dungy's and Tom Coughlin's autobiographies are two favorites.

During the summer before the start of fall practice, Williams had all the players read *The Last Lecture* by Randy Pausch and Jeff Zaslow, in which the author inspired readers to embrace life as he coped with terminal cancer. The players had to write and share book reports at the start of the season. The exercise gave the team a chance to learn much more about each other as they shared their own reflections on the book. The team was apprehensive at first but came to embrace the task later.

"We were like, 'Coach, we already have enough work with school. But we learned to really respect one another," McNeal said.

According to Williams, anything done in the off-season has one goal: to develop relationships based on trust. His team displayed great team chemistry this past year.

During the season, Williams tries to keep connecting to the players by doing small bonding things that could keep the team loose and united. He gave his assistant coaches the night off, rented a small shuttle bus and took the entire team to dinner across town. Along the way, he made a special CD with some of the player's favorite music on it. The team got so into the music that he couldn't get them off the bus to eat.

"They were too busy all singing and dancing to the music," Williams said. "It was a simple idea that had a big impact and one of the best team building ideas I've had."

34. Homer Drew on His Greatest Coaching Job

Former Valparaiso Coach Homer Drew was interviewed the season after his team's magical "Sweet 16" run in the NCAA tournament.

What made that team so special?

We had six seniors on the club. That leadership and experience can't be replaced. The confidence they played with was amazing. This was our third consecutive year in the NCAA tournament. That confidence that knowing we had been here before helped. The willingness to sacrifice was a great part of our success. Everyone gave up a little bit of themselves to make the team better.

103

In regards to the psychological aspects of coaching, are there one or two areas you feel are most important to develop on your team?

Communication is so important. The players need to know what is expected of them, what their role on the team is. Then we look at areas that need improvement. Some may need to get more physical, some may need to be less physical and play with more intelligence.

What's so challenging about coaching is each person is motivated differently. You need to find out what excites each player to help them achieve their maximum potential. That's the key to effective coaching. It takes constant communication.

Do you meet one-to-one very often or mostly just with the team?

Each staff member and myself meet one-on-one with them. I try to get into every apartment and dorm so I'm in their environment and they are comfortable when we talk. We try to spend time with the team and let them know it's not just winning and how they play, but that they graduate and get a good start in life. Helping them develop as a person is very important.

How did you use the movie Hoosiers (about an underdog small town team who overcomes all the odds to achieve success) as inspiration?

We watched Hoosiers on the bus ride before the first tournament game. The theme was that it didn't matter what the size of the school you are from, but the size of the heart in you. In the pre-game sessions, we talked about how important fundamentals are. That's what brought us here. We used some of the analogies from Hoosiers to implement them into our game plan.

The buzzer beating shot that beat Mississippi was practiced numerous times, sometimes unwillingly. How many times did you go over that same play?

In case we had a game ending full court situation, we practiced that play every other day. Sometimes the players would say, "Do we have to do this again? We already know it." They didn't think they would ever get a chance to use it. Now, I'll never have to ask them to practice that play. They will all want to do it from now on. Because of what happened, they know that persistence pays off.

What are the keys to getting the most out of a practice situation?

We start practice with a short team meeting while we have announcements and go over a thought or inspirational slogan for the day, then we'll have a short team prayer. Next during shooting drills we'll play music in the background to get the tempo up. It helps get everyone motivated. Sometimes the players will choose the music.

Do you feel it's appropriate to pray to win or pray for things to go well and no one to get hurt?

It's my belief that you should pray to play to the best of our ability and injury free. I'm not sure God takes sides out there. He has a plan for each one of us and that's what is taking place. I'm most concerned that we play our best, win or lose.

Other than Dale Brown, who were some other major coaching influences?

I think you can learn from a variety of people. After we lost to Indiana one game, I asked Bobby Knight what his focal point on defense was. He told me "to limit Bryce's touches." (Bryce was Valpo's best shooter).

I asked him to tell me how could I get him open against other opponents. Coach Knight took me into a room and for the next 20 minutes he was the ultimate teacher. He brought up ideas on using screens, proper footwork, and other intricacies of the game. Other coaches have also been willing to share. You pick up things from different sources and use it any way they can help your program.

John Madison, Editor www.championshipperform.com

35. Chris Beard on Having a "Street Dog" Mentality

Two hours before tipoff, Texas Tech Men's basketball coach Chris Beard was already coaching. His players were out of position.

"Guys drop your bags," Beard shouted in the hallway outside Texas Tech's locker room Saturday night. His players were about to watch the end of the first half of the Final Four's opening semifinal between Auburn and Virginia.

"No phones. No headphones. No bags," Beard said. "We got three minutes to watch. Take the first minute to look around a little bit."

Even the smallest of details matter to Beard.

As a Division II coach, he'd pick a team like Michigan State or Duke to follow for the season, not because they were on the schedule, but to "follow their journey." How did they react after wins or losses? What were their substitution patterns? How did coaches interact with players? It was a lab to study from afar.

After arriving in Lubbock, he would have each player's keys to shooting free throws posted in Tech's bathroom. Every moment, even one conducted in private, is an opportunity to improve.

"He's wired 24/7," said senior Norense Odiase. "His attention to detail is unparalleled. He grinds it out. He tells us that he's not the smartest, but he's going to out tough you. We all follow after that."

The Red Raider tapped into that contagious energy to reach the national championship game against Virginia and lost in an over-time heartbreaker.

"We have a process that we believe in," Beard said. "It has the academic piece. It has the individual work, the shooting, the team practice, the film, the conditioning, the diet, the sleep — all those things go into our process."

The day before Texas Tech's semifinal victory against Michigan State, when fans could watch the four teams work out for 50 minutes each, Beard ran his team through a 30-second timeout drill.

He sent his starters to the other end of the court, took a few steps toward the scorers' table and formed his hands into a T.

The starters rushed back to the bench. Managers climbed the steps and unfolded chairs on the elevated court. The rest of the team jumped up, clapping and shouting. Beard entered the huddle.

Then it was time to do it again, even more efficiently the second time.

Beard keeps his newcomers on their toes, literally. Players get initiated to the Beard way with a first trip to the hot yoga studio where the team practices a special brand of yoga with his players in a studio where the temperature will exceed 90 degrees.

They have to do things like hold the downward dog pose for nearly two minutes — hands and feet grabbing all four corners of the mat, shoulders and core engaged, hips extended — as sweat begins to drip and arms start to shake.

"It was like 20 minutes in," one new player said. "I was looking at Coach like 'Is this thing almost done.' And he was like 'We got like 45 more minutes.'"

Then there are Beard's sayings.

"He's like a human encyclopedia," Odiase said. "We had a white board at our apartment and we just started writing down funny things he would say."

Beard and his players have waxed on the following topics:

Street dogs: Beard, while accepting his AP coach of the year award, was asked by senior transfer Tariq Owens if he was a dog, what kind would he be. "With all due respect to pet store dogs, I really prefer street dogs," Beard said. "They've got about 48 to live. And they live with a little more urgency, and they understand accountability and discipline a little bit better. They're not entitled because they were in the pound, man."

Smell the roses: Beard's slogan for the Final Four: "That just means enjoying everything, but also then being us when it comes to basketball, and I think we've done that pretty well," he said.

Thankful texts: Beard doesn't want his players looking at their phones, but he will ask them to take them out on occasion to send a message of gratitude to someone in their life: "It's very difficult to go out and be in a bad mood and have a bad practice if you send two thankful texts to somebody in your past."

The secret is in the dirt: Sometimes you have to dig for what you want, it won't always be sitting on the surface.

Clearing your plate: During a team meal, if Beard sees a player hand their plate to a worker, even if they kindly offered to throw it away, "he'll get all over you about that."

"Just because we're having success doesn't mean you can be entitled." Beard preaches a non-entitlement program.

"I'll be a guy that will wake up tomorrow just to try to put ourselves in a position to win," Beard said. "I'm sure when we wake up Tuesday it will be about recruiting and trying to get back. I don't ever want to change who I am."

Excerpted from an article by Chris Fickett of the Kansas City Star.

36. Red Auerbach: Architect of 16 Championships

Former Boston Celtic General Manager and coach Red Auerbach played a major role in 16 NBA titles. He coached the Celtics to 8 straight world titles from 58-66, then transferred into the role of GM where he built one of basketball's greatest dynasties.

As a coach, Red Auerbach was known to get thrown out of a game as a motivational ploy to get his players attention. It often worked.

He created "Celtic Pride," a motivational tool he used to orchestrate greatness in the organization. According to Auerbach: "Motivation is very hard to address because there are so many factors involved. You must pay attention to the little things. One of those was a dress code. Some might ask, 'what good is that?' I wanted my players to have a feeling of superiority and a dress code was where it started. I wanted them to act differently than other teams, to carry themselves better than the guys who showed up for the game in sweatshirts and dirty socks.

If you want to be a champion, you have to act like one. That's all part of motivation. How you conduct practice, the way you teach players to address the media or public, the dress code — the little things all add up.

What are the most important ingredients of a championship team?

The chemistry of the ball club. You can't have too many Chiefs and no Indians so to speak. Getting along with one another and team discipline are important. The team has to respect the guy in charge. They also have to realize that individual statistics mean little when it comes to winning championships."

You were known as a fiery coach who got on your players when the situation called for it. How did you typically conduct yourself before and after games?

"I never cussed out a player in public. I tried to keep my halftime and post game locker rooms disciplined and business like.

Sometimes I started my post game speeches with some humor, then we would get more serious. Sometimes I would start out mad and then get funny. The worst thing a coach can do is talk too much. Then players will start to tune you out. They over-coach. Players get tired of listening to the same statements over and over. I used to pride myself on avoiding repetition. I didn't want them to know what I was going to say."

What are some ways you challenged your players on a day when they were not practicing the way you liked?

"One day I couldn't get (legendary center) Bill Russell to do a thing. He was loafing and so were a few other guys. No matter what I said — it wasn't getting through. I said, 'Can't you guys give me a 20 minute scrimmage where you go all out.' But they wouldn't. So I said, 'That's it. Get out of here. Practice is over. I don't want to see you guys anymore today.'

The next day they are wondering what I'm going to do. Before the team arrived I placed five cigars out on a table. When they got to the gym, I simply said, 'I want a 20 minute practice where we give an all out, playoff type effort. If I don't see it, we're going to do again and again until we get it right. I've got five cigars and no place else to go.' That got their attention and led to one of the best practices of the year.

As far as playing like you practice, there is a tendency to pace oneself at practice, especially once you have solidified your spot on the team. But what happens when you start pacing yourself in practice, you unconsciously start to do the same things in games. Instead of playing all out, you try to pace yourself and pick your spots, which is terrible because there is no substitute for hustle."

What are your thoughts on team discipline?

"Coaches today take the approach that they should be in total control — of every practice and every game. Sometimes, they act like dictators. To get the respect of your players, you treat them like the way you want to be treated. People used to ask me how I 'handled' my star players. You don't handle them — that's something an animal trainer does. You deal with people. If someone has a problem or issue, we would visit one-to- one. We would talk it out and come to a reasonable conclusion. Some coaches today have a total disregard for their players' intelligence. That's a mistake."

What is the best advice you have given to other coaches?

Do some listening. Don't be so domineering that you are the boss every day. Organize your staff and demand excellence, but don't get to the point where you have to prove that you are in complete command at all times.

I also told some of my assistant coaches not to hold grudges. Guys are going to do some things that tick you off. If you get down on a player about something that he has done, don't let those bad feelings linger. Get them out in the open. Lay it on the line.

Partially excerpted from the book "Why We Win" by Billy Packer and Roland Lazenby.

37. Gregg Popovich: Managing an NBA Team with Excellence

In the following profile, San Antonio Spurs head basketball coach Gregg Popovich explained how he handles adversity, how he teaches his players to handle failure and the best organization structure.

According to Popovich, "Is everything going to go your way in life? You think you're on the Earth and everything you want to happen to you is going to happen to you positively? The measure of who we are is how we react to something that doesn't go our way."

Example: When the Spurs lost in the NBA finals 2013, Popovich said he was quick to keep his team from blaming bad luck, telling them, "You're in charge of yourself. There are always things you can do better." The team spent hours reviewing every play from Games 6 and 7 of the 2013 Finals and learning what they could have done better to have won the championship.

Popovich explained how he and the Spurs often talk about entitlement and appreciating their opportunity to play in the NBA: "The notion that you deserve something more than somebody else — that's the most false notion one can imagine. But I think a lot of people forget that. They think that they're entitled to what they have. So we talk about those things all the time. You have no excuse not to work your best. You have no reason not to be thankful every day that you have the opportunity to come back from a defeat, because some people never even have the chance."

Popovich, who is often seen acting grouchy on the court or during interviews, has reached the peak of NBA coaching, putting games into much bigger contexts to improve his players' outlook on life. He has earned the trust and respect of his players. Perhaps the most important part is how honest he is with them:

"Each one is different. I just try to be as honest with them as I can. I just think blowing smoke at guys and trying to manipulate guys or trick guys into thinking this, that and the other, it doesn't work. And it's tiresome. You got to remember what you told somebody last week. And this week, I can't do that because I did that, and now I got to do this. That simply doesn't work. So if you're just brutally honest with guys, when they do well, love them and touch them and praise them and if they do poorly, get on their [butt] and let them know it and let them know that you care. And if a player knows that you really care and believes that you can make him better, you got the guy for life. Being honest with players, riding them when they're bad and praising them when they're good, earns their trust and respect."

His winning style of play and player management has helped make the Spurs one of the model franchises in all of professional sports. Popovich discussed how to keep players motivated and how to handle the personalities throughout the season. He explained that being honest and holding people accountable is the best way to see results. "I think you have to have accountability. For us, the thing that works best is total, brutal, between the eyes honesty. I never try to trick a player or manipulate them, tell them something that I'm going to have to change next week."

Example: He handles his star players the same way he does his bench and that philosophy keeps the team a tight-knit unit.

"If it's Tim Duncan and it's a timeout and I don't think he's doing what he should be doing, I'll ask him, "Are you gonna rebound tonight? Are you gonna rebound at all? Or are you just gonna walk up and down and then we're gonna go to dinner? What are we gonna do here? And he'll listen and then he'll walk back out on the court and say, 'Hey Pop, thanks for the motivation.' And a lot of coaches are afraid of that. They want the best players to like them all the time. It won't work. It'll bite you in the bum after awhile. You need to have the same standards for everyone. You can treat people differently because each one is different, but they all have to march to the same drummer, to the same standards."

Popovich explained that character — namely being able to handle criticism — is important and allows him to be more upfront with people: "If you're on Duncan's fanny or Parker, [other players] see it and they know it's fair and they wanna play for you. And it just compiles geometrically, and it just keeps going and you end up having a really good situation."

Popovich has helped build a strong, enviable culture in San Antonio. While on-court talent has played a big part in that, the culture and dynamic set by Popovich and the Spurs front office can't be overlooked. They have a winning culture, they adapt to their personnel, and they create a working environment that encourages both teamwork and individuality.

Defending champion Golden State Warriors GM Bob Myers keeps a Popovich quote from 2014 stored in his cell phone to remind him of how good teams are supposed to function: "A synergy has to form between the owner, whoever his president is, whoever the GM is, whoever the coach is. There's got to be a synergy where there's a trust. There are no walls. There is no territory. Everything is discussed. Everything is fair game. Criticism is welcome, and when you have that, then you have a hell of an organization. That free flow through all those people is what really makes it work. And that includes everything from draft to Xs and Os. Nothing should be left to just one person – it's a collective effort or the culture doesn't form."

Excerpted from the Business Insider magazine. www.businessinsider.com

When you are speaking with your team after a win, never talk about the kid who was the star of the game. Talk about what your other players did to help you win the game. Be sure to spread the wealth. Then have individual meetings with one or two players to praise and reinforce what they did right. Make sure you high five or put a hand on the shoulder and make eye contact.

MIKE KRZYZEWSKI (COACH K)

38. Jay Wright: Straight Shooter Leads Villanova to Greatness

Long time Villanova basketball coach Jay Wright has led the team to two NCAA titles in his 20-year career at the school.

The night before home games, Villanova basketball coach Jay Wright and his players stay at a local hotel. The team eats a meal together and watches video of the next day's opponent. And then the coach dispenses a little insight — along with bottled water and a healthy snack — before everyone heads for bed.

One such night this winter, with his top-ranked team seemingly on a cruise control, Wright stood to address the players. As usual, he began by plunging a dagger into the group's collective ego.

"Being ranked number one?" Wright says. "It's BS. We haven't played teams like Kentucky or Kansas. It means nothing. This season is all about dealing with the 'disease of me.' You're 22 years old, and you're walking around campus and everyone is telling you you're a rock star, which is why I'm inspired by you seniors, because you work to get better every day."

Thankful as he is to be winning, Wright seems perpetually attuned to a subtle frequency of worry — to an internal signal reminding him of the precariousness of the human psyche. He wasn't always this way. When he became a head coach at Hofstra in the mid-'90s, he obsessed over the game strategy. He thought, as many coaches do, that the intricacies of play design and the sheer force of his will were the lone keys to winning.

But after three losing seasons, Wright's job was in jeopardy. His team would invariably lose close games by unraveling when setbacks occurred. A late three-pointer by the opposing team might demoralize his team on the next play. Maybe, he thought, the difference is *attitude*. If his guys could learn to be unaffected by the last play, and to play for one another rather than for the adulation from the stands, maybe they could get out of their own way.

And so Jay Wright embraced a new approach that emphasized how his players *thought* about the game, and he brought it to Villanova in 2001. These days at the team's facility, there's ample evidence of Wright's focus on the psychological.

"See, we think about every message they hear and see," he said, pointing to phrases painted everywhere, slogans like *'Players play for their teammates and coaches; actors play for the crowd.'*

"We're not complex in what we do X-and-O-wise," he said. "But we do **spend a lot of time on how we react mentally to every situation.**" The idea isn't to draw up lots of plays but instead to give his guys the confidence and the freedom to make plays. And here is where Wright's psychological approach feels unique. While just about every coach in America rallies his or her players with motivational verses or tries to summon an inner dwelling Tony Robbins, Wright wants his players to feel as if they're in control on the floor, admonishing them to play with a "free mind."

Tough Love with Josh Hart. One day a player came to Wright's office and told him he wanted to be a 3-and-D kind of player.

"A 3-and-D guy, what's that?" Wright asked.

"All I gotta do is hit threes and play defense and I'll play in the NBA," Hart told his coach.

"I went off on him," Wright said. "I was telling myself, 'This kid's gotta trust you, so don't lose it with him.' But I couldn't help myself. I told him that sounded like some BS an agent told him, someone looking to make money off him. I don't want you coming out of here just hitting threes and playing defense. I want you to be a complete player. I kicked him out of my office. I was sure it was the last thing the kid wanted to hear."

Each year he has performance consultant Jim Brennan administer a character test that he calls the team's 'Rosetta stone.'

"One thing about Josh that the personality survey points out is that he does not like to disappoint people he cares about," Brennan told the coach.

Brennan, who also consults for the U.S. military, thinks Wright's approach with Hart represents a kind of reverse engineering: "We believe *selfishness* isn't natural, that human beings evolve into selflessness if given the chance."

That's why, at the team's practice facility, there are no championship banners or retired jerseys, no photos of Villanova greats in the NBA peering from the rafters or from the walls.

On the court, Wright is interested in how his players relate to one another, which means practicing things you might not expect. If a Wildcat takes an offensive foul or dives for a loose ball, the other four players are expected to run to him and help him up. Similarly, if a player hits a big shot in a game and gestures in celebration to the crowd, he'll incur the wrath of Wright, who spends as much time policing his kids' public displays as diagramming plays.

Wright doesn't mind when his players are demonstrative on the court — he just wants the enthusiasm directed toward the team. "If you're excited, you have a lot of energy; turn and give that energy to your teammates," he said. "Not the crowd"

With Brennan's help, Wright has focused his players—and himself—on paying attention to what they're experiencing, urging them to "Be Here Now."

Excerpted from a GQ magazine article by Larry Platt. www.gq.com

39. John Wooden's Coaching Philosophy

Long time sport psychologist Dr. Rob Gilbert (RG) went one-on-one with Coach John Wooden before his passing. What follows are highlights from that interview.

RG: Is winning overemphasized in athletics today?

Wooden: When you are in competition, you should make every effort to win in the proper manner. I think winning should be based more on making the most of what an individual has to offer. **My definition of success is peace of mind which comes through the**

self-satisfaction of knowing you made the effort to become the best of which you are capable. That was always my philosophy. You can't find a player who played for me that he ever heard me mention "winning." However, I was constantly imploring them and exhorting them to make the most of the abilities they had. They are losers, regardless of the score, if they do not make the most of their own abilities. These talents may not measure up to the same standard of someone else's, but if they have done their best, it is a success. A student in a class is not a failure when they don't make an "A," if the best he could do was a "C." Many games are lost, simply because the other team is better than you are. There were times when I considered our team a failure when we let a clearly inferior opponent even get close to us. So winning must not be based on scores or a position of power or prestige. It is like reputation or character. Character is what matters – not reputation. Character is what you are – reputation is what others think you are.

RG: What are the positive aspects of losing?

Wooden: Losing gives a realization that there other people and teams better than you. It brings you down to earth sometimes. If an opponent did not have the physical qualification that you have, but were better prepared and won the game – they were victorious not because of their ability, but because of your failure to capitalize on your own ability. This reality can be brought up in a positive way. I had a little saying I would tell my teams:

Remember this your lifetime through. Tomorrow there will be more to do. And failure waits for those who stay ... with some success made yesterday. Tomorrow you must try once more ...

even harder than the day before.

Remember, the better you do, the more eager the opponent will be to topple you. Therefore, it is logical, you are going to have to continue to do well. This means always trying to be the best you are capable of.

RG: Is there any benefit to "psyching up" players before a game?

Wooden: For every peak, there is a valley. If you use some type of artificial means to stimulate your players to rise to great heights – there will later be a corresponding valley they will get in to. I think you should constantly be exhorting your players to make the most of what they have and stay as close to their peak level of competency as much as possible. This should be regardless of the strength of the opposition – whether they are inferior or outstanding. I tried to have my players never show any excessive celebration over a win or did I want any excessive dejection because they were outscored by another team. I would tell them to hold their heads high, as long as they made the effort to play as well as they were capable.

RG: It was reported in Psychology Today magazine that you used twice as much negative reinforcement as positive reinforcement. Do you feel that was valid?

No. I believe that the researchers were too far away from the court to understand. Most of my instruction was of a positive nature – a pat on the back or setting a positive example of how to do something. I would not let the researchers down on the floor. They sat

123

in the stands and may have heard more negative stuff because it was something important I was addressing. **For example, I might speak more firmly when I was emphasizing something. When I complimented – it was directly to the individual. When I corrected, I wanted everyone to hear.**

RG: What are some of the psychological aspects of coaching you felt were most important?

I constantly tried to make players realize the mental side of the game. You can't go out and play consistently at a high level simply because you have the physical qualities. The person who does not discipline himself is going to be at a disadvantage. This discipline can take on many forms – it can be mental, physical or moral. Any person in a position of leadership has to constantly study those under his or her supervision. Realize that no two people are alike. You have to work with individuals in different ways. I didn't believe in trying to change a person's core make-up. For example, you are not going to make a fighter out of someone who is not made that way. You might be able to for a short time, but the results will be fleeting. I don't think you can make someone into something he is not. You must make every attempt to have players realize and understand themselves and their strengths. They just constantly study and analyze themselves to realize what they are capable and not capable of.

RG: What advice would you have for a young coach planning to make coaching his or her life's work?

First, I would study those in the profession who have done well. I would find out exactly what made them do so well. I would read all that others have written about them and what they have written about themselves. I would also seek out the advice of another more experienced coach who has a personality that might resemble yours. Maybe you are a Bobby Knight type or maybe you are Tom Landry type. Find out what they have done and study their methods and procedures.

At coaching clinics, I would tell younger coaches to read as much about psychology as they could and take some courses in the subject as well. Since you are working with people, a coach's success is going to depend on how much you can get out of those under your supervision. You have to not only be an expert about the sport you coach, but you must know how to get along with others – regardless of their personality. Do not think you are "handling" people, you are working with people. They are not things. So the two most important things you can do is study those in the profession who are successful and learn psychology to be more successful working with others.

Dr. Rob Gilbert is the author of "Read This Book Tonight to Help You Win Tomorrow",
published by Championship Performance. www.championshipperform.com/books

40. Coach K on Leadership Essentials

The following chapter on Duke Men's Basketball Coach Mike Krzyzewski (Coach K) discusses his approaches to team building and leadership culture.

At a Duke basketball practice, 150 executives watched as Coach K put his team through a fast-paced high intensity practice – which included running drills and pulling players aside for one-on-one, eye to eye talks. Tim Jeffries is one of the attendees who liked the way Coach K handled his players.

"I see my job within the scope of a team. I was impressed by how hard he seemed to be working on building trust with his players. That's a total key to success in my environment," Jeffries noted.

Basketball seems to more fit today's corporate environment which is also fast fluid and requires great flexibility. Players must make decisions on the court rather than waiting for orders from the sidelines. In both business and basketball, the question is how to manage in a way that employees/players make smart decisions, work together, and ultimately succeed.

Coach K holds his hand in the air to display his five-point leadership plan that includes *communication, trust, collective responsibility, caring and pride.* Individually, each is important. Collectively, they are an unbeatable combination, Coach K says as he makes a fist with his five fingers.

In Coach K's perspective, five players who come together can beat five more talented players who don't. "The fist is a great metaphor that keeps the guys focused on what we're about as a team," Coach K said.

Though he is a West Point graduate, Coach K advocates a surprisingly unregimented approach to management. He resists hiring "yes" men as assistant coaches, doesn't enforce hard and fast rules, and in practice does not use a whistle. He feels that using one would put distance between him and the players.

While Coach K has had a long run of success, a back injury he incurred during the mid-1990s taught him how important cultivating a culture of leadership among assistants and team leaders really was.

"While I was away recuperating, my business got away from me. The whole situation made me realize that I needed to delegate more leadership responsibility to my assistants and team captains. The program's infrastructure was not as strong as it needed to be," he said.

Coach K employs former players as assistants to help sustain the leadership within his program. They fill the role of mentor to his players.

According to Dr. Robert Keidel, author of *"Playing Ball in Business: Management Lessons from Team Sports,"* successful managers must take lessons from various sports depending on the situation they face. At different times, managers can take a top-down authoritative approach used primarily by football or ice hockey coaches, delegate authority such as a baseball manager or collaborate which is most common with basketball coaches.

Mr. Jeffries took home some lessons and immediately called a meeting with his seven top managers: "I told them I trusted them to do their jobs well. I told them to take prudent risks that will result in failure from time to time. In the long run, that philosophy will really help us achieve greater success."

Coach K emphasizes team building and team play, brand awareness, goal setting, resource management, and building and sustaining a quality product. But he often puts an unusual spin on these mainstays.

When speaking to a business audience, Coach K tells executives that the key to Duke's basketball success is the hard work, mental toughness, and the "heart" demonstrated by his players.

Like any good coach, Coach K isn't afraid to give his players a good 'tongue blistering' when it's needed.

"This isn't all about 'I love you,' and 'Let's hold hands and skip,'" he said. "It's also about 'Get your rear in gear,' 'What the hell are you doing?' and 'Why aren't you in class?'"

His nontraditional philosophies are well illustrated by a statement some coaches would shy away from: "**Too many rules get in the way of leadership and box you in,**" Krzyzewski says. "I think people sometimes set rules to keep from making decisions."

He also doesn't focus on number of wins: "I never set number goals. Never. Goals that focus on playing together as a team are more important and can position your team to win every game.

Success is doing the best you can - all the time. As a result, you are able to define what success means to you. It's a real mistake to let others define your success."

Coach K's organizational ideas are very important. When his players report to their first team meeting of the year, they don't just get uniforms – they also receive notebooks, pocket calendars, and other logistical items. Then Krzyzewski give his time management talk. "We teach the students about time management as it relates to them individually and also as a group. We want them to know right off the bat that they also have responsibilities to their teammates."

He promotes team interdependence in a variety of ways. For example, early each season he gives players a card with all their teammates' and coaches' home phone numbers and encourages them to stay in touch with and help understand one another. While he has recruited his share of "stars," he says he doesn't bring them onboard based on technical merit alone. "It's equally important to consider how they might work as part of a team," he says.

And once he has recruited a good group, he works to earn their respect by being "caring, communicative, and honest," Coach K says. "Your team needs to instantly believe what you say," he tells business leaders. "That's why you have to heartily embrace the concept of personal responsibility."

Coach K encourages leaders to capitalize on their strengths: "If you're daring like Bobby Hurley, or confident like Christian Laettner, or humble like Grand Hill, use it to the fullest," he says.

His own strength, he believes, is his ability to get inside his players' heads and hearts. "An important part of being a leader is the ability to feel what your players or employees feel," he says. "I do a lot of feeling, and my guys know it. I can't dream up plays and defense without knowing how Shane Battier and Jason Williams feel. And it makes me a better coach."

The first question he typically asks CEOs is: "Have you connected with your people lately?" He, too, has difficulty staying on top of that one as demands on his time continue to multiply, he tells them.

"You have to work at it, because, ironically, the success that your business enjoys tends to pull you farther away from your people," he says. "I tell business leaders that the first sign that you have a good team is the existence of trust. The team that trusts – their leader and each other – is a good team to lead and is more likely to be successful."

The self-described 'teacher and coach' tells executives he prefers to be called 'influential,' rather than powerful.

"I think it's more important to be influential, to possess the ability to have people listen to you and follow you so that you can help bring about positive change."

"Leadership is getting people to buy into something, making them feel vested in the whole decision-making process," says Grant Hill. "Coach K is remarkable at doing that."

41. Billy Donovan on Individual and Team Motivation

NBA and college basketball coach Billy Donovan has led the Florida Gators to two national titles and four Final Four appear-

ances. The University of Florida has renamed the court in his honor.

One of Billy Donovan's favorite books is '*The Precious Present*,' by Spencer Johnson. It takes little effort to figure out the book's moral — that living in the moment is the key to happiness. It takes considerably more to do as Donovan has done and live that message every day. He asks his players to forget the last game and not look to the future. Can they live in the present?

"It is wise for me to think about the past and to learn from my past. But it is not wise for me to be in the past. For that is how I lose myself." — Quote from the 'The Precious Present.'

Two weeks into his tenure at Florida, Donovan told his assistant coaches: "I think we can win a national championship here."

It meant taking a mediocre program to the sport's highest level. Donovan started by recruiting quality players with reputations as hard workers – and persuaded them to come build something. A run to the national title game followed in 2000.

In 2006 and 2007, he achieved the dream with back-to-back national titles. Then came a few down seasons with no NCAA births. His 'live in the moment" mentality kept them from dwelling on the disappointment of those NIT years. The Gators learned to focus on each day and not what had happened before.

"My past was present. And my future will be present. The present moment is the only reality I ever experience."— The Precious Present

Depending on whom you ask, Donovan's success comes back to one of a few things — his work ethic, his focus on the mental aspect of the game and his ability to recruit and motivate players.

AD Jeremy Foley said Donovan's work ethic hasn't changed. Each day demands complete focus on the task at hand. 'Right now' has become his catchphrase for the year, and players give a knowing smile when asked how much Donovan focuses on that.

"He says that almost every day, in practice and games," said center Vernon Macklin. "And it's the truth. We must live in the moment. We can't think about the past, can't live in the future."

In the offseason, Donovan seeks feedback from other coaches. He never feels like he has it figured out, and makes sure his players know they don't, either.

"He always wants to undress what we're doing and see if he can find another way, or find a crack and remove a weakness," said assistant coach Larry Shyatt.

All the while, Donovan is equal parts psychologist and motivator. Ask him about why his team struggled in a win and he's more likely to give an answer about why his players didn't handle the "human element" than why they struggled against a 2-3 zone.

What did you learn from Rick Pitino (who Donovan played for at Providence)?

"He wanted feedback constantly and he created chemistry. He

squashed egos and got guys to buy into the team and his system. Coach Pitino took an active interest in my life away from basketball. I always felt like he cared. I don't want any of our players to ever think that I don't care. If they think I don't care, then I've done a poor job spending time with them away from the practice court. There are things going on socially, academically and in the basketball world, that can prevent them from playing up to their ability, so knowing them as a total person helps with motivation."

Discuss some general thoughts on motivation.

"It's our job as coaches to find out how each player is motivated, what makes them tick and obviously try to go about handling them the best way we can to get them to fill their obligation to the team. Some guys, I have to bring in the office and talk to them one-on-one, others need to be brought out into the crowd.

When you're dealing with a team, I don't think you can just say this is the way we're going to do things. I've got to try and find ways to get each guy to fulfill their responsibility by understanding who that person is as an individual.

Times have changed. When I was playing in high school and college, there was a separation. I never dreamed about going into a coach's office, sitting down and shooting the breeze. You just didn't do that. Maybe there are certain coaches who still try to keep themselves at that distance level — who don't want to get too close to the players.

I have no problem with a kid coming in here, joking around with them and having a good time with them away from the court. I want them to feel good about themselves, and to know me, and for the relationship to be something that after they leave here, there is a relationship beyond player/coach, to consider me someone that will be there for them. At the same time, I'm not going to tolerate anything less than those kids giving me their best every day."

(In the off-season as he put the players through their paces, strength and conditioning coach Scott Webster wore a Gonzaga Basketball t-shirt as a daily reminder of who knocked Florida out of the previous year's tournament.) Do you think it is productive to remind a team of a past failure to motivate?

"Coach Webster came in and checked to see if he could do it. I told him I had no problem with it. I think we needed to be reminded of that game. You want that in the back of their mind as they're working out. Those guys got a little taste of the NCAA Tournament last year. So you want to remember Gonzaga, not to dwell on it, but to understand through past mistakes, this is what we've got to do to put ourselves in a better position."

You have brought in an array of sensational talent. How do you keep all these heralded prep stars content? How do you establish team harmony and unity and get kids to accept their role?

"Everybody needs to be treated fairly, everybody needs to be treated the same. We have certain rules on our team and if those rules are broken, regardless of whether you're the leading scorer or the last guy on the bench, you're going to be treated the same way.

However, you have to realize you're dealing with a lot of different entities, a lot of different individuals, therefore each individual is motivated and plays the game of basketball for different reasons.

If I look at it, as everybody's the same, every personality's the same, that's where you run into trouble, and you probably aren't maximizing coaching that young man if you take the personality out of it. You have to understand you're dealing with 11 entirely different people and everybody's motivated differently.

Our freshmen came in and were very, very humble. They gave our upperclassmen a lot of respect, and I thought those two ingredients gave our team very good chemistry. Our guys put winning as the most important thing. The unselfishness and guys understanding their roles — that's why we won. That's the important thing to me, guys putting winning first and foremost."

The team concept was equally embraced by the younger players.

"If people were worried about individual statistics, they wouldn't come to Florida," said one former player. "We play too many guys, we're not going to put up big numbers — nobody on our team is going to lead the SEC in scoring, assists or rebounds because we don't play enough."

One season, highly touted freshman Brett Nelson started to play like he was out there all by himself. In high school, Nelson knew if he didn't take control of a game, it didn't get done. But he got over that and started to blend in nicely with the team.

"My whole thing is winning, whether I play two minutes or 40 minutes," said Nelson. "The main thing about this system is that it's very unselfish. We try to make the extra pass and make our teammates better."

Now that Florida basketball reached new highs, how does the team deal with expectations?

"You want the bar to be raised. I don't get that concerned about expectations among media people and fans. I'm more concerned with expectations of myself, the expectations of the coaches on ourselves and our kids. And when you can talk about being the best, that's good.

I wish that during my first year at Florida, there were more expectations placed on our basketball team. That first year team felt they weren't supposed to win, especially against top ranked teams like Kentucky or Arkansas. That's the difference between top-notch programs like Kentucky, Duke, and Kansas and everybody else. They expect to win — they expect to be there every game.

There wasn't much I could do about the situation. I could sit and look 'em in the face and tell 'em (they could win), but I don't think they'd believe it. Winning makes guys understand everything they're going through, there's a purpose and a method behind the scheme. The preseason conditioning, the practices, and the amount of time that's put in — it's for winning. Certainly once you have some success; it builds confidence within the team, and creates an excitement and enthusiasm level."

John Madison, Editor www.championshipperform.com/books

42. Pat Summitt: Deep Dive into Coaching Methods

Tennessee women's basketball coach Pat Summitt will be remembered as one of the all time greats of women basketball. She led the Lady Vols to 8 NCAA championships and 18 Final Four appearances. In the following profile, we look at her approach to coach/athlete relationships, team discipline and motivation. This chapter is written in present tense to reflect her coaching methods at the time.

On communication: Coach Summitt would meet with each player four times per year to discuss everything ranging from player goals, fears and ambitions to the role that is expected of her from the coaching staff in an effort to really listen to and understand her players. Summitt also regularly communicates with her players in writing short notes that may offer encouragement, express concern for players' well-being, or remind players not to take her on court criticism too personally. Summitt believes the written word has a permanence that makes an impact on players in ways that the spoken word cannot.

Another dimension of communication is Summitt's demeanor on the court and off, and the importance of adjusting her tone and modes of communication to various situations. Summitt's roles range from speaking to players as confidante and advisor, or as a teacher who must communicate in a severe voice to get the student athlete's attention, and as a coach who yells out blunt, straightforward commands in tough game situations. All three situations require different modes of communication and Summitt stresses that "circumstances must dictate how you need to speak, or whether you need to shut up and just listen."

On Team Discipline: According to the coach: "Discipline is all about structure. It is the bare-bones architecture of your organiza- tion, the beams and joists that hold everything together. Maintaining the integrity of your interior philosophy is crucial. Even if it costs you a valued member of your team. Otherwise your structure will collapse."

In the past, Summitt has dismissed key players from her teams and believes it is right to do so if "the values and credibility of the entire organization are at stake."

Summitt has described how she has developed a system of team discipline in which after four years, upper classmen become the disciplinarians of the team. All team members are accountable for the actions of each other, so the group has a stake in the conduct of each individual. This way, Summitt has to do very little punishing or penalizing her athletes. The structure of discipline becomes self- perpetuating, and if applied with consistency, provides a clear cut, unambiguous formula for success as the team journeys together in pursuit of a common goal. In this respect, she is careful to distin- guish discipline as a much broader concept than punishment, which she views as only a form of "temporary behavior control."

According to Summitt, "Discipline is a comprehensive form of conditioning that requires repetitive, consistent drilling and is required to accomplish anything of real quality, whether in sports, music, or academics."

On Motivation: Coach Summitt once kicked the Lady Vols out of their palatial locker room for five weeks and squeezed them into a tiny visitors' dressing room. She felt they hadn't deserved the palace. They hadn't worked hard enough.

At the end of a three-hour practice, she times the suicide sprints on the big scoreboard clock. She films every practice and then sits through it all over again, so that if a player decides to question a single one of her criticisms, Pat takes her right to the videotape in her office and stops the thing so often to prove she's right that it takes an hour to cover the first ten minutes.

After the Lady Vols fell apart in the second half of a home game, she had the team go straight to the locker room and hang up their uniforms. The next day she had them put on those smelly uniforms that had been locked in the trunk all night. She called for a scrimmage to make sure they played the second half they didn't play the night before!

But Pat knows when to pull back as well. One time she forced an All-American player to the breaking point. In tears, the players had told Pat she was killing her love of the game and while she wasn't going to quit, Pat had to back off.

The old Pat maybe wouldn't have adjusted, but the new Pat is a little more flexible. She lightened up on the player and the Vols went on to win a national title later that same season.

On Player Coach Relationships: Coach Summitt can come across as intense, authoritative, certain, and yet so caring. When she walks into a room everything about her — her ramrod posture, her confident smile, her steel blue eyes and her direct manner of speaking, seem to imply, "I love what I'm doing and this is what I'm here to talk about. You'll pay attention while I'm talking to you or you'll leave the room."

A typical practice can find Pat challenging her players. Suddenly in the midst of a seemingly good practice, Pat might shout, "Hold it! Stop! Everyone stop!"

Here is a sample conversation that follows:

"Lisa!"

"Yes Pat?"

"What have you done for your team today?"

"Well, uh ... I ... I don't know."

"That's exactly my point! Now everyone get back to work!"

One minute she turns players' names into an obscenity on the court, then walks off it and becomes like a mom to them in the post practice meeting.

During one-on-one conversations with players Coach Summitt will invariably ask what the player thinks the team needs to do to win. She will ask so intently that it seems as if the two of them are the only ones in the universe. After commanding total respect, Coach

Summitt will turn around and have her players call her Pat.

In a huddle with 20 ticks left in a tie game, she will make a decision, kneel on a stool in front of her players and pull them into her dead sure eyes. The Lady Vols will drink in this calm, assurance and intensity. As they walk back onto the court, the players know that their coach has just given them the way to win. They can almost feel it.

On time management: All Tennessee players are required to carry day planners, opening them together at Pat's command to fill up a stray half hour here, a vagrant hour there, even to transcribe her annual reminder in late October: 'Don't forget to turn your clocks back one hour!'

She watches tape of her opponents while she works out on the treadmill, while she's scribbling "POINTS OF EMPHASIS" on a notepad, while she talks on a phone to her assistant. *Lesson: Pat definitely practices what she preaches.*

Some of Summitt's coaching methods included the following:

1) Demands players sit in first three rows of classes and forbids them a single unexcused absence. If you miss a class, you won't start. It's that simple. Skipping class means you will be on the bench for tip-off in the next game. The "no class, no practice, no play" rule means that if a player fails to show up to a class, they do not practice that day, and then they do not play in the next game. They still must always dress out and cheer each of their teammates the entire game.

2) Makes it a point to find out about every visit her athletes make to the mall, restaurant, or movies — and always mentions it the next day in conversation.

3) After end of a 3-hour practice, she times the "suicide" running drills on the big scoreboard clock to motivate her team.

4) Films every practice (reviews each one and uses it to prove her words of criticism if a player disagrees with her).

5) Everybody on team is responsible for a loose ball. Otherwise, she will force players to sit in a sitting posture — without a chair.

6) Once after a loss where the players performed poorly, Coach Summitt has been known to make players put on smelly uniforms that had been locked in the trunk all night for practice the next day.

7) A pre-game ritual before conference or NCAA tournaments is to show the team a highlight tape cut to music. On mounted TV screens throughout the bus, the team will watch sequence after sequence of themselves in action making great plays to music like "Catch Us If You Can."

8) A comical moment: Before a Final 4 game, there was a strained air in the pre-game locker room. "In some ways, a semifinal game can have more pressure than the championship game. So, I decided to take some advice from one of my players and 'loosen up.' I teased my hair straight up from my head. It looked like I had been electrocuted! They caught it on camera. I told one of our players, 'Hey Chamique, this is what I look like right before the game when

I get really nervous!'"

Coach Summitt adapted well to changes in players and differences in the team's chemistry over the years. Here are some other notable quotes from her coaching philosophy:

On rules: "The implied intent of any rule is, 'This is a priority!'"

On confrontation: "I don't tell people what they want to hear, I tell them what they need to hear."

On success and failure: "For 24 hours, enjoy a win and then move on. Nothing is as good or bad as it seems."

On perfectionism and expectations: "I guess I am a perfectionist. You don't get what you expect. You get what you demand."

On what she will say at her last team meeting: "Take everything you have learned from each other and on the court and take these life skills with you so you can be successful."

Kay McDaniel, Asst. Professor Lee University

43. Gail Goestenkors: Coaching Psychology for a Successful Program

College basketball coach Gail Goestenkors led her teams to 17 consecutive NCAA tournament appearances, including four Final 4's with Duke.

What psychological aspects of coaching do you consider most

143

important and why?

Understanding that each player is motivated differently. To accomplish that, you have to get to know the player and find out what's important to them. Some players need to be yelled at, while others will shut down under the same treatment. Finding that balance is key. The team must also understand that we each have different personalities and we are motivated differently. They need to know that I will push individuals in different ways for the good of the team.

I read an article that said you have put together highlight films of the team's best moments as a motivational tool. Are there any other creative ways you have found to motivate your team in the past?
When we played a regular season game at Georgia Tech, I took the team to the Georgia Dome (site of the Women's Final 4). Our theme last year was "One Team, One Dream." We went inside the Dome and I told them to get comfortable with the surroundings. We had five freshmen on the team who I wanted them especially to see what it was like. I talked about the dream and what it would take to make it happen.

If an athlete gets into a shooting slump, but her technical form is fine, what would you say to that player to help her recover?

First, I would give them more personal attention. I would start to shoot with them. I would give positive reinforcement, "Don't worry — you are a great shooter," while I'm shooting with her. I would play some fun shooting games like horse, where they can relax and not think too much about their slump. This way they won't stress out as much about their shot. Generally, if the form is fine, but you struggle, confidence is an issue. The game then becomes stressful. I want the game to become fun again. They usually get their confidence because they can beat me. Then we'll put together a highlight tape of them making shot after shot. That will help them regain their confidence and touch of when they were shooting well.

Are there any particular team building exercises you have used that have been consistently beneficial to your team over the years?

When they get back from summer, we do show and tell — just like you did in kindergarten. Everybody has to bring something from home that means something to them and something that the team doesn't necessarily know about. Five minutes before each practice session, we have a different player do their show and tell. This brings the team closer together. They're sharing themselves and they're childhood with each other. It's also nerve-wracking for the freshman when they get up there for the first time. It gives the rest of the team empathy because they've all been in that situation where you're speaking in front of the team for the first time and you're sharing part of yourself with them.

We have them do book reports. Players have to stand up in front of their teammates and kind of put themselves out there and talk about what they have learned through the book. I probably have about thirty books that we have used over the last couple of years.

Are they mostly sports related or about any subject?

Anything, but mostly sports related. "It's Not About the Bike," by Lance Armstrong is one of my favorites. There are basketball books like "A Season is a Lifetime" by Duke Men's Coach K and "Values of the Game" by Bill Bradley which are great.

Short books like "Who Moved My Cheese" or "The Precious Present" can be read very quickly. In cases like that, I'll assign them two books. We assign the books to players depending on what we think they need to hear.

For instance we gave "Who Moved My Cheese" to a freshman because she was very rigid in her ways. She needed to become more flexible and understand that there are other ways to do things. It was good because after she read it, she said, "Okay, now I get it." She knew exactly what I was trying to get at with her. Since we've read all the books and know the themes, we sit down as a staff and decide which book will be assigned to which player.

Are there any other exercises you have found build team unity?

We have a trail that's around the golf course that we run — it's about three miles. It's good for conditioning because it's very hilly and mentally and physically challenging. We do that run during the preseason, then again during the season at some point. We say, "It doesn't matter how fast you go, it's about team and we're all going to cross the finish line together." They do the run on their own and they have to stick together as a group. Everyone stays at the same pace. The run is harder on some than others.

For instance, last year one player really struggled the most with the trail. So the rest of the team said "Okay, you (the player) are going to lead us and we're going to follow." They knew the only rule I had was that they all had to come in together at the same time. It didn't matter how fast or slow they were. So the player who usually struggled ran her best time because she wanted to lead the team.

When you first came to Duke, the resources aren't anything like you have today. What advice would you say to a coach who is trying to build a program with limited resources?

Work ethic is essential, because you have a lot of ground to make up. Doing things the right way. There are no short cuts. Never lose your integrity. Regardless of resources, the personal touch is always most important. Don't be afraid to be creative.

How do you help an athlete balance all their academic and athletic responsibilities while they are in your program?

We start off with eight hours of required study hall for all freshmen. The freshman year in particular is a tough adjustment, so learning time management skills are very important. The eight hours of study hall is held in the academic center — just one floor down from my office, so it's perfect because it's in the same building we're in. There is someone in charge and the players have to sign in and out. There are tutors in the study hall room they can meet with. I have two coaches that are in charge of the academics. They both oversee a couple of players. The kids have to turn in their grades every week. The two coaches have a copy of their syllabi so they know when they have a paper due and can ask, "Okay, where's the first draft, where's the second draft?" — those kind of things.

Especially here, the academics are difficult so we know we need to make sure they start off well to help their academic confidence level.

Do you give them any time management training at all?

They have someone that comes in and speaks to them early on about time management, about test taking, and those kinds of issues. There are so many resources available. During the first month they have at least one meeting a week with someone who is here to try and help them.

When you're talking to someone who is feeling pressured and stressed out, is there any advice you can give to a student athlete like that?

When they are feeling overwhelmed, we tell them to write down everything that they are doing within a day. Find out where they are wasting time and where they can be more productive. Instead of coming over to Cameron (the training facility) on three different occasions, let's get you over here once to do your practice and your study hall and your weight lifting all at the same time as opposed to three different trips. Usually you can find some time that's been wasted. Watching Jerry Springer in the afternoon is not real productive. (Laughs)

Can you discuss staff relationships and keeping productivity high?

Every year we change responsibilities. That helps coaches not get too comfortable or get in a rut. A different coach is in charge of recruiting each year. I have coaches move up with a class — that helps with relationship building. I also want my assistants to become head coaches if they desire. I need to help them become very well rounded. We all share scouting responsibilities. I make sure they don't scout the same teams each year.

What are the most important elements of being a successful recruiter? Are there any "sales strategies" that get prospects excited during official campus and home visits.

We're very genuine with the recruits. We don't try to make things better than they are. I always try to speak from the heart when I talk to players. I don't tell them what they want to hear, but I am truthful with them. Kids can tell if you are just 'blowing smoke', so be honest.

How about strategic aspects of recruiting?

We meet every week as a staff and decide who is going to call what prospect for the upcoming week. I'll call every other week and have one of my assistants call in the off week because I want them to get to know the entire staff. They need to get to know me best since I will be making the decisions once they get here.

Besides being academically and athletically talented, what evalua- tion criteria do you use to evaluate high school prospects?

Besides talent, work ethic and attitude are very important. We learn about the prospects by talking with them, their parents, and their coaches. Checking out what kind of relationship they have with their parents and coaches is important. We talk with the school guidance counselors as well to see if they will be able to handle the academic responsibilities.

John Madison, Editor www.championshipperform.com

44. Pat Riley on Building an Enduring Championship Culture

Pat Riley led the LA Lakers and Miami Heat to 5 NBA Titles. In this interview, he discusses the 'disease of me' and what it takes to build a championship winning culture.

How can teams blend their individual strengths into a focused, cohesive unit?

People are territorial animals. We all want to stake out something we can call our own. We strike back when our turf is threatened. We all want to protect what we have. Those instincts can be positive, but only when they are harnessed for the good of the team.

The key is to reclaim innocence. I'm not talking about being soft. Being innocent means understanding the territorial nature and knowing that each player has his or her space, but when you know it will harm the good of the team, you put aside your individual agenda.

Innocence is an attitude that comes from inside. What a lot of players don't recognize is that doing the most for the team will also help them grow as individuals. Teams don't just come together. It takes patience and a willingness to get to know the deeper aspects of their teammates.

What are your thoughts on the player who sacrifices for the team, but doesn't see any tangible benefit?

They may think to themselves, 'what am I getting out of this unselfish play?' Not all teams behave fairly. It's how a player deals with what happens to him or her that counts. Good people sometimes get screwed in the process. It's so important to grow from these tough experiences.

I have a saying: **"It doesn't make any difference what happens to you, it's how you deal with it. Learning how to deal with adversity is what really counts."**

It's important to get away form the mindset that says – "my teammates owe me something." We live in a world of failure messaging. In any seemingly hopeless situation, there is always a chance for rebirth. A player's survival instincts will defeat their territorial instincts. Being part of a successful organization is more important than being personally indispensable.

You talk about team building being an "innocent climb." Please elaborate from your past coaching experience.

An innocent climb in its early stages is a fragile thing. There are negative reversals, before heading in the right direction. It's back and forth, not a straight up deal.

Most people in this world don't want people they are in competition with to get better. To break this cycle, it starts with a more innocent attitude of wanting others to get out of the game what they desire, not just my own development.

Example: Magic Johnson was a dominant player, but he realized early in his career that as the man controlling the ball, he could help his teammates get the most out of their abilities. Michael Jordan had to learn this same concept before he could lead the Bulls to their titles.

The biggest battle in high-level basketball is the one between style and efficiency. Being more efficient in performance wins most of the games. Style can juice a player or fire the crowd up, but it doesn't win games.

Discuss what you refer to as 'the disease of me.'

One of the worst things that can happen to a young athlete is that they experience a ton of success early in their playing career. This type of success can breed a 'me first' attitude.

The Lakers won a championship in 1980, but they were not a champion organization. To make this transition, they had to overcome the great barrier that is the disease of me. This disease can strike any team at any moment. You can bank on this and you must address it head on and get rid of it. Otherwise, the selfish attitudes will tear at the fiber of a great team.

The disease of me is ever present, but it can be overcome and anticipated. During and after the 1980 season, hidden agendas were taking shape that signaled an outbreak on the team.

It started with an injury to Magic, who was out for three months. The public address announcer would always remind the crowd that, "Magic will return to the starting lineup February 27." While the organization was eager to get Magic back on the court, they forgot about motivating the guys that were actually getting the job done in his absence on the court. Don't think all those players didn't hear those announcement and similar press articles and start to feel like they were not appreciated.

Magic's return was the beginning of the end. The Lakers became a divided team. Resentment and envy became a by-product of selfishness. We forgot about teamwork, togetherness, equality, positive attitude, role meshing, and being kindred spirits battling with one heartbeat.

Some of Magic's teammates had come to resent him. Our game focus went to hell. In a make or break situation during a deciding playoff game, we gave an uninspired effort. We lost the game because two players failed to communicate on a simple defensive switch.

It was the disease of me coming to its inevitable result. It was a horrible feeling. To lose to a team you know you were better than because of self-inflicted destruction caused by greed, pettiness, selfishness and resentment was the worst.

Going forward, we learned to recognize the symptoms of the disease of me and how it affected our play. By being able to address selfish play and agendas before they could cause great damage helped us sustain nearly a decade of greatness.

How did you turn around the team's attitude and lay the foundation of future success?

People have often asked, "Which would you rather have – a winning team or a together team?" When you understand team dynamics, the answer is obvious. A team first must be like a family. Strong covenants are forged in crisis.

During the 80/81 season, the Lakers operated with the unspoken agreement that stated it was ok to put the team second, just because you felt wronged or jealous. That kind of team attitude is the quickest way to sink fast.

It was a downbeat off-season, but one in which we forced all the 'dirty laundry' out in the open. Nothing was off the table including discussions about Magic's new contract, complaints over lack of playing time, and the type of offensive and defensive systems we would run. Lots of open wounds were brought out from beneath the surface.

When hidden agendas were brought to light, after the supply of scapegoats were totally exhausted, we finally began to sow the seeds of trust. We asked for every player to give out at least one compliment during each day's practice to a teammate. This was a simple exercise to start acting positively toward one another. Soon the barriers to creating an enthusiastic team were overturned.

We established a team covenant with the goal of creating equal footing by assigning responsibilities that would gall on each individual player's shoulders. We also made a list of terms about how each player could do his part to support his teammates. This was a critical foundation building block for success.

Talk about the importance of having a core identity in your program.

On the first day on the job when I took over the Lakers I wrote on a blackboard: **"A house divided against itself can't stand."**

I told the team there would be no more dirty laundry handed out to the media. We had to behave like a family. A team that is loose, happy and trusts one another usually performs best.

The leader's job is to create an environment where all can flourish. You have to know when to push hard and when to back off.

Each team needs a core covenant, which has to evolve into an unspoken agreement. We had to make it a clear conscious contract that included a commitment to each other. We had to learn to tolerate differences of opinion. We had to get into the spirit of unity and togetherness. Not just one and done. We had to work at it again and again as true team building involves trial and error.

Every team must decide very consciously along the way to uphold covenant terms that represent the best of a team's values. Examples include, cooperation, love, hard work, concentration, and putting the team above ourselves. Everyone on the team had to decide now: either you are in or out.

I told them: "As a team, we have set standards that we think will make us a make a championship team once again. As your coach, I will be the enforcer of the rules you set and the covenants we all establish."

This exact moment transformed me as a coach and I never looked back. The forging of a strong covenant involves positive peer pressure that intensifies any team's performance.

Talk about your approach to core team covenants.

Covenants can only be energized in an atmosphere of total trust. I enforced the standards and told them that any criticism should be taken as a sign of confidence and caring. I would be tough to make you better.

When you have a shared core covenant in place, the team is together. It is together in organization and attitude. You want every team to be put on a road to uninterrupted success. But life is never that smooth. Bumps in the road happen. As a coach, you always need to be ready for that. Thunderbolts of unexpected problems will test the character of your covenant. Teams with high character can weather the thunderbolts and learn to embrace them over time.

Inner winners build a sense of anticipation that minimizes any kind of adversity. Sometimes when adversity strikes, we rail against that fate and lash out at the people around us. True winners never play the role of victim. They don't say, "There was nothing I could do.

It was meant to be. I will go hide in a corner somewhere until somebody helps me."

A Riley rule on beating the sympathy of this: **Giving yourself permission to lose will guarantee one thing – a loss.** If you don't toughen up, that is exactly what will happen.

Example: Let's say a player is coming off an injury. Now that player has an excuse not to go hard. That's an excuse to lose. Out '83 Laker team had three starters out with injuries for at least a month. This destroyed our attitude and will to win. We all silently decided if anyone had the right to lose, it's us.

Instead of focusing on the talented bench we had, we allowed adversity to rock us and we mentally gave in. We assumed the consequences of losing somehow wouldn't fall on our shoulders. With that kind of an attitude, it was easy to understand we lost 4 straight games in the finals.

This experience taught us all a very valuable lesson: if you are going to be a championship team, you have to be one under all conditions. You have to think championship thoughts all the time. The "it's ok to lose" mentality or attitude is a prescription for disaster.

You can ground the thunderbolts of disruption by involving team leaders. Exploit the equivalent benefit of any adversity by trying to milk as much personal development as you can out of the situation.

Coming back from a thunderbolt has little to do with grand strategy. It has a great deal to do with strength of heart and the conviction to follow a basic plan and stick with core principles.

Refuse to accept the thunderbolt has the power to ruin your team. Half the battle is overcoming the "I can't" or "We can't" mindset.

Can you discuss the relationship between preparation and choking?

Failure at a critical moment can come from either overestimating your own strengths or from not believing you have what it takes to get the job done. Choking is always a miserable experience, but by no means does it have to be terminal or cause long-term damage to a player or team.

Choking one game or single moment does not brand your team as permanent losers. It does mean that you have something to overcome. It could be a psychological barrier that needs to be addressed or a lack of preparation.

Regardless of sport, to beat the other team you must study them and find any weak points to attack. You have to be totally prepared. A player who is just physically prepared, but not mentally ready increases the risk of defeat and is a liability to the team. Players would always come up to me after practice and say, "Coach, I'm ready to play. Start me or give me more minutes."

I knew every player's practice habits, state of mind and overall attitude. Many times I would look them directly in the eye and say, "I know you think you are ready, but you are not fully prepared."

A lack of confidence can be like a self-imposed performance cap. The only way to increase confidence is to increase your level or preparation. This is the whole key to avoid choking.

John Madison, Editor www.championshiperform.com/books

The essence of Core Team Covenants is totally positive peer pressure. It replaces blaming and finger pointing — two vicious enemies of teamwork — with mutual monitoring and mutual reinforcement. Positive peer pressure intensifies any team's performance and brings it closer to peak.

PAT RILEY

SECTION V

Motivation and Coaching Psychology

45. 25 Ways to Say "Well Done" to An Athlete

1) You're on the right track.

2) You're really working hard today.

3) Exactly right.

4) I'm proud of the effort level today.

5) Keep working it. That's the kind of improvement I want to see.

6) You're a bunch of fast learners.

7) Keep it up – you're making my job enjoyable.

8) One more time and you'll have it right.

9) You're getting better every day.

10) Keep up the good work.

11) Nothing can stop you when you bring that kind of intensity.

12) That's better than the last time.

13) First class effort (guys or ladies). Keep it up.

14) That's the best I've seen today.

15) Much better than yesterday.

16) That's how we handle that situation.

17) Right on target!

18) You're really improving.

19) You did a lot of great work today. I'm proud of the effort.

20) I've never seen better execution of X drill.

21) You all outdid yourselves today.

22) Finally, I think you all got it.

23) Good job (insert player name).

24) Finish strong.

25) Championship level effort.

46. Two Coaches on the Psychology of a Big Comeback

When the Belmont men's basketball team trailed Campbell 75-57 with less than four minutes to play, most observers thought the game was over. They were wrong. Belmont mounted a furious rally and stunned Campbell 87-84.

According to retired Belmont Coach Ricky Byrd: "The mentality of the two teams in that situation is entirely different. When you have that big of a lead, you don't want to shoot too quickly and you don't want to foul. You almost have to play conservatively. It's a sense of protectionism. On the other side of the coin, we had to play with a sense of urgency. We had absolutely nothing to lose."

To help win the game, Belmont tried to get Campbell out of their tempo and played very aggressive defense in an effort to create as many turnovers as possible. A little luck didn't hurt either as Campbell missed 11 of 18 free throws down the stretch.

Former college basketball coach Seth Greenburg says that coming back from a big deficit involves both psychology and strategy to get a "W": "You've got to paint a mental picture for your players of how you are going to get them back in the game. You show them a scenario where they can cut a 16-point lead to fewer than 10. Then from 10 to 5 in a certain amount of time. If you can convince them to continue to compete when they are down a large margin and get a few big stops, you can pull it off."

47. Concentration, Keywords and the Attentional Field

Concentration is often a misunderstood factor in athletic success. Typically, people think of concentration as the ability to focus on one thing for a long period of time. It is much more complex. To understand concentration one must understand the *"attentional field."* This field includes everything within and without a person they could focus on at any given moment.

These would include external sights, sounds, smells and internal thoughts, emotions and physical sensations. Good concentration may be characterized as focusing only on performance relevant aspects of the attentional field or those things necessary for good performance. Poor concentration involves focusing on things irrelevant to performance. For example, thinking about the fans, the speed of opponents, the size of the trophy, etc. distracts an athlete from what their focus should be on – performing in the moment.

Generally, there are two styles of concentration. 1. *Internally focused.* These players tend to think too much and ruminate on their thoughts and feelings. This obsession is often negative and hurts performance. Before game time, they like to go off by themselves and sit quietly. This type of athlete needs to work on directing attention outward to keep them from thinking too much about the competition.

2. *Externally focused.* These players tend to concentrate too much on external cues in the competitive environment. They are easily distracted. They constantly interact with others. For these athletes, it may be more effective for them to focus more on performance-

relevant information such as quietly visualizing the upcoming event.

Recommendation: Coaches can assist players in developing a keyword that can be repeated to remind them of what they need to focus on. Using keywords has a twofold benefit. First, since athletes can't think of two things at once, if players repeat keywords to themselves they eliminate distractions. Second, using keywords constantly prompts players to think of something that will help them play their best. **Keywords can be motivational "go," technical "block" or psychological "calm."**

Coaches can help players identify the most crucial factors for good play and then devise keywords to focus attention to that specific area. To boost the effectiveness of keywords players may want to write them down on a wristband or bat or racquet, etc.

An alternative to this approach is to identify a key object to focus on. Key objects stand out in the athletes "attentional field"; therefore they are easy to focus on.

For example, hitting their thigh with a fist provides a noticeable physical sensation and acts as an effective focusing tool. Another effective focusing tool is simple breathing. When a player is distracted, coaches can tell them to take several slow, deep breaths. This focused breathing relaxes the body, which results in a broadening of concentration and redirecting of focus away from anxiety. Concentration is also shifted from distracting thoughts.

Jim Taylor, Ph.D www.drjimtaylor.com

48. Keep a Winning Attitude During a Losing Season

Down years. Rebuilding seasons. Injuries to key players that turn a great team into an average one. How can you keep your athletes interested and motivated during losing seasons?

The key is to give athletes other "small victories" and other chances to win in different ways. Winning teams overcome obstacles. Most of the time the primary obstacle a team or athlete is measured against is the opponent.

How can individuals and teams win when the scoreboard says they lost the game or match? One method is to create different obstacles and let the other team be part of your "game."

Example: A tennis coach whose team had lost 4 straight matches devised a plan. Since the skill level of his players was weak, overcoming certain obstacles during their matches was their way of "winning." If a player got 70 percent of their first serves in, they considered the match a success, no matter what the final score was.

Example 2: An undersized basketball team was getting beat quite handily by their bigger and faster opponents. The coach decided to focus on their free throw percentage and field goal percentage. On defense, she noted how many points each opponent was averaging and if one of her defenders limited that opponent to less than her average, it was considered a victory.

By using different criteria to judge performance besides wins and losses, athletes can feel they have gained or accomplished some-

166

thing in a losing effort. Small "moral victories" boost confidence. Motivation increases when the player feels they have something to play for other than a championship or title.

Note: It's important to never accept losing as inevitable. That's a destructive mind set as well. But during the rebuilding process, small victory steps lead to greater future rewards.

What are other methods of motivating players during a losing campaign? Find something after each loss and tell the team what it was. Never accept sloppy practice or lackadaisical play which leads to a "we're going to lose anyway mentality." This type of thinking will never allow a team to turn things around.

Another idea includes changing practice schedules. Occasionally let team captains plan a practice or encourage them to develop new drills for technique work.

From your standpoint, never give the impression that you have lost hope or given up on the team during a tough season. You may have to look harder, but there are silver linings in losing years.

One last area to consider here: What about the player who gets depressed, even to the point of feeling worthless during a losing year? Particularly with women's teams, self-worth spirals down with each successive loss.

Remind these players that the self-thoughts of "winning" athletes are defined by how close they came to reaching their potential during the season. This is how they should evaluate their performances instead of only looking at wins and losses.

If they perform consistently well in a losing effort, you are in the best place to analyze shortcomings. Goals may have to be adjusted, but the athlete's self-esteem is still intact. Process, rather than outcome, goals are important during these types of years. It helps keep wins and losses in proper perspective.

49. Control Eyes and Ears for Better Performance

Note: The following chapter is addressed directly to athletes.

Controlling eyes and ears is the key to stay in the right mental time and place. Before and during a game you should only look and listen to those things that keep you calm, confident and ready to perform to your full potential. The free throw shooter who focuses on the rim before her shot or the rower who stares at a spot in the middle of a teammate's back are controlling their eyes. The player who listens to his or her favorite music before the game or the wrestler who pumps himself up by telling himself everything he's done to prepare are controlling their ears.

The inability to control your focus is what causes and prolongs down periods of performance. By learning to control where you focus your eyes and ears before and during a performance, you will be well on your way to busting any slump.

Controlling your eyes means locking your visual focus of attention on specific, prearranged points before your performance. Where you focus your eyes is especially important when there is a natural stoppage in the flow of the performance, such as timeouts, breaks between halves, or time between races, events or shots. It is during these non-playing moments when you have plenty of time to think that you are most vulnerable to a performance disrupting loss of focus. In all sports, the more time you have to get into your head, the more creative ways you'll discover to set yourself up for failure.

If focusing your attention on friends in the stands pre-event helps keep you centered, then continue doing this. If looking into the stands or at your opponents makes you uptight, don't do it. Instead, find somewhere else to deliberately focus your eyes.

Examples: Watching your legs as you stretch them, picking out one spot and staring at it, looking at your shoes, and focusing on your glove are all examples of what you can do to control your eyes. By picking specific targets to look at ahead of time and regularly using them, you'll have a much easier time staying calm and confident when it counts. These focal points will distract you from real distractions.

Using the same focal points repeatedly will contribute to your comfort and confidence, because anything familiar tends to ease anxiety. It's the unfamiliar that causes athletes to get too anxious to play to their potential. Having a familiar target for your eyes in these new and stressful situations will minimize chances for choking.

Often thinking where not to focus can hinder performance. Self-coaching, such as "she's right next to you – don't look at her" or "don't think about how strong he is," only serves to keep athletes focused on all the wrong things. Having a specific visual target for your eyes enables you to control attention in a more constructive way.

Controlling your ears entails listening to only those things that keep you calm, confident and ready to perform your best. To control your ears, you must monitor two sources of auditory input: sounds coming from outside yourself like the crowd, a teammate or trash talking opponent and from inside yourself, your self-talk. Some athletes repeat specific affirmations to themselves before they perform or during breaks. One athlete would say to herself, "PCP" several times in her mind before the start of the race. PCP stood for *powerful, confident, positive*. This helped her neutralize the tendency to think about her opponents' strengths or wallow in the negative.

Dr. Alan Goldberg Competitive Advantage: www.competitiveedge.com

50. Twenty True/False Statements to Determine if an Athlete is in a Slump

The best insurance an athlete can possibly have to avoid an impending slump in performance is an awareness of the early warning signs. When an athlete can identify the early stages of a slump, he or she can take action steps to defuse them.

In his book *Sports Slumpbusting*, sports psychologist Dr. Alan

Goldberg has developed a 20 point questionnaire that helps athletes tell if a slump is heading their way. The 'slump meter' is based on a series of general questions that athletes should ask themselves periodically before and after a performance. Each statement represents a potential mental mistake that a slumping athlete can make. If they start to regularly commit too many of these type of errors, watch out, a slump is most likely on the way.

Here are the 20 True and False questions athletes can ask themselves:

1) The harder I try, the worse I get these days.

2) My self-talk before this performance was negative.

3) I was dreading the performance.

4) My concentration during the performance was in the past or the future.

5) I couldn't get over how strong, fast, big or talented my opponents were before the start of the event.

6) I kept seeing internal images of something bad I was afraid would happen before the game.

7) Before the game, I was upset by something that had happened earlier in the day.

8) My self-talk has a lot of 'Here we go again' and 'This bleep always happens' and 'I never' statements.

9) I found myself evaluating and criticizing my performance while

it was going on.

10) I worried about failing before and during the performance.

11) I was singing the what-ifs before and during my performance.

12) I feel incredibly frustrated by my performances lately.

13) I focus on mechanics and instruct myself a great deal during performance.

14) I was not enjoying myself at all during my performance.

15) I found myself carrying around my mistakes the entire game or competition.

16) I kept remembering past examples of lousy performances.

17) I'm having trouble remembering the last time I had a decent performance.

18) I seem to be trying too hard lately.

19) Even though everyone says my problems are mental, I'm still convinced it's my mechanics.

20) I find myself thinking way too much during performances.

Conclusion: The athlete should add up the number of true statements (honesty is very important here - editor). Now they can rate themselves on the slump meter.

0 to 2 means their mental state for peak performance is in near perfect condition.

3 to 5 indicates the athlete is holding his or her own and not in any immediate danger of getting in a slump.

6 to 9 is a warning of trouble ahead. 10 or more reflect increasing amounts of dangerous slump thinking, which is most likely to precede an actual slump.

Dr. Alan Goldberg www.competitivedge.com

51. Case Study: Sport Psychologist Works to Improve Basketball Program

A sport psychologist (SP) worked with a European basketball team to help them do well in competitions leading up to Olympic qualification. This chapter examines some of the techniques the SP used to help improve the team.

The main objective was to prepare players for specific games. Special attention was given to developing tactical and psychological skills for both individuals and the team. One of the goals was to help players mentally cope with the heavy load of games in the European leagues.

Specifically, the SP wanted to help players improve competitive stress levels, enhance pre-game routines, help players remember tactical plays to be used in upcoming contests, develop total concentration, and positive affirmations for before and after contests. "Homework" assignments were given for players to follow up after practices.

During the season, the SP would address specific game concerns for specific players. For example, the head coach was planning on increasing the playing time for a backup center. The coach asked the SP to spend some extra time with the player to prepare him for this challenge.

In another case, the assistant coaches didn't feel the two guards were communicating well enough on the court – either in practice or games. The SP conducted a specific session where he tried to help each player improve his communication skills. (Editor's note: In a situation like this, the SP or coach could role-play various situations the team might face.)

Example: Ball is turned over when point guard's pass is intercepted. Besides hustling back on defense, what will the guards say to each other during the game that doesn't tear down the teammate who made the poor pass?

Example 2: The team failed to perform well in the final two minutes of the last game. A group discussion was held where each player gave his opinion on why the offensive plays that were run during that stretch didn't work. What specifically was wrong based on your film review or to the best of your memory? What could be done better the next game to improve when faced with the same situation? Once successful strategies were outlined, players were asked to imagine executing the plays to perfection.

In this phase different tactical plays were introduced on a weekly basis. The SP used imagery training to help the players better remember those plays. For example, during a typical session players would watch video prepared by the assistant coaches showing players performing various offensive and defensive plays correctly. The player would watch a short video clip of an offensive trip down the court, then it was shut off. Players were then asked to visualize themselves executing the plays. They were told to reinforce the visualization with self-talk that helped create a more vivid picture in their mind of them running those plays.

The group sessions in season were comprised of weekly "state of the union" meetings where each player was asked to share his thoughts and feelings about the practices and games during the previous week. Players were encouraged to react to what their teammates were saying. Coaches were not present at these sessions.

Coping skills and how players cope with the tactical load that was placed on them were two prominent topics. Players were grouped by position to discuss how to improve. For example, the centers and power forwards discussed how they improve decision making on the court and then were asked to use imagery for both offensive and defensive plays. In one case, the players discussed the principles of the particular zone defense that they had performed in the previous game. The exercise helped them realize that they were not performing the defense to the level they needed to. The players outlined specific errors they were making. To improve the zone defense, the players imagined themselves performing the defense to perfection, stressing the key individual and team elements to effectively carry it out.

During these discussions the SP encouraged players to express themselves and exchange ideas.

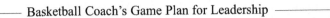
If you can improve players' self-esteem and confidence, get them to relax, teach visualization and routine, they will shoot as well, or better, with the pressure on.

JOHN CALIPARI

52. Pushing Through Training Barriers

In the following chapter, sports psychologist Alan Goldberg talks about how athletes can push through training barriers instead of settling for lesser goals to reach a higher level of performance.

Why do athletes have a problem with settling for lesser goals instead of pushing to a higher level?

The first thing a coach has to do is help that athlete get in touch, with what's called the "Big Enough Why." They have to know why they are training.

Too many athletes try to trade what they want the most for what they want right this minute. They say things like, "I don't want to go to practice." or "I'm really hurting right now, I want to back down." As a coach, you have to keep the athlete connected to their "Big Enough Why."

They have to take that "Big Enough Why" into practice. They have to understand what they do today is going to make the difference whether they reach their long term goals or not. Athletes often lose sight of that connection between training and success.

It's the coaches' job to help an athlete have a breakthrough. They have to get them back in touch with why they are doing what they are doing. They have to communicate their own belief that the athlete can accomplish what they have set out to accomplish.

What is the coaches' role in this process?

Coaches have to take responsibility and remind athletes why they are doing what they are doing. Give them the impression that they can get beyond what they might think. Sometimes athletes start doubting themselves. Help them believe that they can do a little bit more than they think they can. Push them. This involves the concept of getting comfortable with being uncomfortable. If you want to get good at anything, you have to get into the habit of continually stepping outside of your comfort zone. People who stay in their comfort zone go backward.

Let's take endurance training as an example. When your lungs are burning and you want to quit, if you quit then, you are giving in to that urge to get comfortable. When your lungs are burning, athletes must stay with the training just a little bit longer. Stay with the discomfort. That builds endurance.

What about athletes moving to the next level — high school to college or college to professional?

Every athlete deals with normal feelings of inadequacy: "Do I belong here?" or "I'm not as good as everybody else."

For example, when a kid comes to Olympic trials for the very first time, they feel completely out of place. I tell them, "Great, you are supposed to have those feelings. This means you are moving up to a higher level of competition and you belong with the best." Every kid is different. The coach makes a judgment on the physical potential and talent level when they first see them. Whether the

178

athlete is living up to his or her potential can be tough to determine. When working with athletes, are there certain signs that an athlete is not doing their best or training up to the max? Sometimes a kid says one thing and does another. They may say their goal is to make all conference, then their behavior says something very different. That's the most visible sign.

Another sign to look for is the athlete who just doesn't walk the talk. They will make excuses for themselves. They might say things like, "the weather sucks today, the wind was blowing too hard" or "the field conditions were terrible" or "the officials used Braille to make their calls."

A general sign is the athlete who won't take responsibility. To get comfortable with being uncomfortable, the athlete has to take responsibility for the success of their training. If an athlete is not doing what they should to get to the next level of performance, it's almost always a matter of them not taking responsibility.

John Madison, Editor www.championshipperform.com

53. How Athletes Can Let Go of Mistakes

Jimmy deftly dribbles down the court, beats his man, fakes out another, then stops and pops ... but he's way off the mark.

Instantly you can read the results on his face and in his posture. He hangs his head as he retreats on defense with the coach's screams of *"C'mon think, damn it!"* echoing in his ears. He's still preoccupied with this missed shot when his man gets around him for an easy score. Now the coach really has something to yell at. Jimmy seems angry as he gets the ball just past mid court on his team's next offensive try. He drives down the lane but he's forcing too much. He flattens an opposing player who has already established position on him and is called for an offensive foul. Then, the coach angrily takes him out of the game.

When a basketball player, or any athlete for that matter, makes a mistake, has a bad game, or lets the team down, one of the most crucial tasks he or she faces is being able to quickly and totally let go of the mistake or poor performance and get right back in the game.

Too often players like Jimmy get tangled up in a bad call or the coach's criticisms and are unable to mentally return to the action at hand. Such a preoccupation with the past has two major effects on performance.

First, it destroys concentration. When a player's full attention, which needs to be in the present (either on the ball, a cutting teammate, or the defense) is instead partially diverted to the past, he or she becomes less sharp mentally and physically and therefore vulnerable to making more mistakes.

Second, getting hung up on a past mistake tightens the ball player physically so that his or her muscles stop working efficiently. This translates into slowed down foot movement (a tense ball player is a slow ball player), and limits mechanical abilities (skating, jumping, or throwing suffers and shooting accuracy declines.)

180

Great games and peak performance in almost all sports come only when the ball player is totally immersed in the present moment, when he or she is not distracted by thoughts about past foul-ups, bad calls, or the coach's reactions.

A common outstanding characteristic among champion athletes is the ability to let go of the bad shot, stupid play, or lousy first half, and get right back into the game.

Summary: We can learn from our mistakes and therefore there is a time that we should think about what went wrong. However, the time is not when athletes are still playing! After the game is over, fine. That's when they should sit down and critically examine recent performances.

Recommendation: During the game, always stay focused on the present play, one play at a time. Your players may find this difficult to do. Certain events or situations predictably "push their hot buttons." For example — having a cold hand, getting roughed up, the coach yelling at them, bad calls — all can distract athletes from focusing on the job at hand. There is a way for them to practice "letting go" and returning to the next play. Have your players make a list of their so called "hot buttons" and next to each, write down two strategies they can use to effectively handle each situation.

Example: If their hot button is getting roughed up without a foul being called, your two strategies might be to: 1) Change self-talk. Instead of focusing on the opponent and how angry they are at him or her, your players can talk themselves into staying calm and alert. 2) Concentrate more intently on their role in the next play.

Once they have two strategies outlined they can practice, through visualization, being in a game situation, having their hot buttons pushed and coping effectively with the distraction so that they can immediately return to the game. Sufficient practice in this way will soon transfer to the game situation.

P.S. Remember, it's not the mistake, bad break, or poor perform-ance that will hurt your players, but how long they choose to hang on to it! When athletes let go of mistakes quickly, you'll see much improved results.

Alan Goldberg, Ed.D. www.competitivedge.com

54. Six Ways to Deal with Competitive Distractions

Note: The following chapter is addressed directly to athletes.

Distractions are a common cause of performance lags in many sports. They can come in all shapes and forms. It can be a com-ment made by someone else, weather conditions, or how we talk to ourselves. In any event, distractions can create inconsistencies in performances and keep us from achieving at the level that we are capable of in our sport. All athletes seek that "can't miss" feeling. Confidence is a crucial ingredient in achieving this and making consistent improvement in performance. If we become distracted, our confidence lags and our momentum is diminished.

An athlete came to me complaining that he could not play in damp or rainy conditions. Obviously, it affected his approach to his game and his performance suffered. Over time, by assisting him to focus away from weather conditions and back to the essentials of his game, he was able to divert himself from the very things that were getting in his way. He realized that during rainy conditions, he tended to become more hurried and confused and he failed to account for the needed changes in his game consistent with the weather conditions. This created variations in performance and frustrated him greatly. By assisting him to become more focused on mechanics, physical requirements and skill required, he was able to gain more confidence and his preoccupation with weather diminished. This is a typical example of how distractions may affect performance.

All athletes are diverted from reaching peak performance by distractions at one time or another. Coaches need to take the time to help players identify their distracters. This is the first step toward improvement. Once the problem is pinpointed, the following suggestions can help develop greater confidence by focusing attention away from both external and internal distractions.

Recommendation: Here are seven ways to deal with competitive distractions.

1. *If possible, practice frequently and keep sessions short.* If you practice too long, your concentration span becomes shorter and you may become easily distracted and less alert.

2. *Add variation to your practice routine.* At times, we all get into ruts with our practice routine. It can become so regimented and mechanical that any benefits fail to translate to the always unpre-

183

dictable demands of the actual sport. Work on different types of body movements and mechanics and by becoming more versatile you will be less susceptible to distraction.

3. *Use positive self-talk.* Forget the last time you choked. Chastising yourself with negative type statements only interferes with your performance and becomes a distraction. According to research, such negative thoughts can divert your attention from your game for as long as 9 minutes every time you do it.

4. *Write down positive self-statements in a log and read them daily.* Such statements should be made in the present tense, such as, "I am well prepared," "I expect to play well." Use a system of goals that are not only motivating but create the discipline both in training and during competition. Write down your short term and long term goals and determine what rewards would satisfy you once the goals are obtained. The more focused you become on reaching goals, the less distractions can get in your way.

5. *Act confident.* Poor posture and a tentative gait can not only cue your opponents to your weaknesses but it can also cue your body and mind to play in a less confident manner. Practice your "game face" and "confidence walk" in the mirror. It is often necessary to "fake it until you make it" until you achieve the level of confidence you find comfortable and visualize yourself playing the way you expect to.

6. *Visualize.* Imagining that you are in a bubble, a tunnel, or wearing blinders, can be highly effective in filtering out potential distractions. Practice using such imagery during practice sessions and

184

while playing your sport. Some athletes utilize the image of distractions as arrows coming toward you then deflecting off your "bubble." Try different images until you find one that works for you.

The main thing to remember is that we all encounter distractions but they do not, however, have the power to control our game unless we let them. Mental focus is the key to reclaiming control over the elements.

Dennis B. Sprague, Ph.D.

55. Coach K on How Specific Words Motivate

In the following chapter, Duke basketball coach Mike Krzyzewski (Coach K) discusses his thought on maximizing individual player motivation and the importance of word choice.

I believe that my work is as much about words as basketball. Choosing the right words to say to players is no less important than picking the starting lineup or court strategies. My primary task is motivation. How can I get a group motivated, not only to be their individual best, but able to become a better team? I have always said that 'two are better than one, but only if two can act as one.'

After the 1999 season, several of our top players left Duke early. I told Shane Battier that he would need to emerge as a team leader, but there was one problem: he never saw himself as a "team star." After the players had gone home for the summer, I gave Shane a call.

"Shane – this morning did you look in the mirror and imagine that you were looking at next year's conference player of the year?" He laughed and said, "Coach I …"

The next day I called again. "Shane, it's Coach. When you were on your way to work this morning, did you imagine scoring 30 points in a game this coming season?" He laughed and began to respond and then I hung up.

Seconds later Shane called back and told me not to hang up on him. I told him, "I won't hang up on you if you won't hang up on you." Shane needed to imagine these sorts of things to become the player he was capable of becoming. He had all the tools necessary to become a great player, but he fully realized his potential only when he allowed himself to imagine great things.

For motivating Shane the crucial word was "imagination." For others, it may be "poise," "enthusiasm," or "self-confidence." Undefined words are meaningless. Dictionary definitions usually do not suffice. Meaning is understood by seeing a word in action. For example, I ask teams to understand the meaning of "dependability" by telling them the story of my brother Bill. He never missed a day of work fighting fires in Chicago for 38 years.

I talk about "willpower" by sharing the story of former player Steve Wojciechowski and his last game on the court. He only scored one point but his sheer determination that day led our team to an exciting victory.

I convey the meaning of "courage" by telling them about my friend, the late Jim Valvano, who used his own battle with cancer to raise millions of dollars for cancer research.

My hope is that, as players listen, my brother's example may remind them of the most dependable person in their own lives. Learning from Jimmy V, they may recall a time when they witnessed true courage.

When an audience makes these associations, we have found common ground. We are no longer merely exchanging words; we are being mutually motivated by their meaning.

•   •   •

Once when his team needed a lift during an uncharacteristically poor season, Coach K invited the whole squad over to his home. He left the room where the team was and came back with boxing gloves on and a towel draped over his neck. He proceeded to throw some punches in the air. His message, while seemingly silly, had a profound impact on at least one player.

"He looked just like a real fighter. It was non-stop energy. It was one of the coolest things I've ever seen a coach do. He immediately lifted our spirits," said former Duke captain Jon Scheyer.

One of Coach K's famous gestures is to make a fist to his team – symbolizing five players coming together as one unit on the floor for greatness.

Coach K has very few team rules. However, he does want all his players intensely focused on collective greatness. When he coached the US Olympic team, he had all the players sign a contract. The contract didn't specify the goal of winning. Instead, it asked that each player be committed to one another and make a full effort on behalf of the country.

His aversion to rules came from his experience playing for the US Military Academy: "The rules I went to school under were never my rules. I definitely didn't agree with all of them," he said.

The military experience underscored for Coach K the need to be flexible and that was tested when he became national team coach. He had to find common ground with NBA stars who have reputations for having supersized egos. Coach K opened up his coaching style somewhat.

"What you want to do is not say, 'This is what we are going to do period.' Instead, you say, 'This is the situation. What do you think?'"

According to Derrick Rose, "He would say to us, "Are you telling me you wouldn't dive on the floor for a ball for the whole USA? When he put it that way, it meant a lot. Most people look at him and think he is very strict. But he lets the players play free."

56. Three Strategies to Increase Motivation

Motivation is a powerful, yet tricky beast. Sometimes it's easy, and you find yourself working with someone wrapped up in a whirlwind of excitement. Other times, it is nearly impossible to figure out how to motivate your athletes, and you have to pull them out of the death spiral of procrastination. The trick? Have a variety of tools in your "motivation arsenal."

Here are three strategies to help build motivation and increase commitment.

Strategy #1: Telescopes, microscopes, and reverse engineering.

The biggest mistake that leads to breakdown of motivation and commitment is that people fail to understand how their end goal can be traced back to today. You've probably heard the advice to set challenging "stretch" goals. While that's great advice, setting big long-term goals seems overwhelming to many people, causing them to burn out before they see significant progress.

The key is to break down big goals into smaller steps, connecting "someday" to "today."

The telescopes, microscopes, and reverse engineering process help *identify* long-term goals. You can then break these down into a concrete, daily process and routine to follow.

Here's how it works:

First, talk about the "telescope" goals that your athlete has and get them all down on paper in chronological order. You can go as far out as they wish. Typically, I try to do 90 days, six months, nine months, one year, and five years. The telescope can see as far as

189

they want to go, but at the same time, we don't want to overwhelm them.

Once you have those clear telescope goals, reverse engineer them to what you can do TODAY to get closer than you were yesterday.

We often refer to these as "microscope" goals. These micro, daily goals should be followed up on a predetermined, consistent basis to check in and provide accountability.

This is a strategy that can be used with all athletes, but **it works best for people who get overwhelmed by thinking about the amount of time and work it takes to reach long-term goals.**

When you help break it down — showing them a small step they can take today and how it directly contributes to their long-term goal — everything seems more manageable. It's the start that stops most people, and excellence in small things leads to excellence in *all things*. Accomplishing the DAILY microscope goals will lead you to your telescope goal.

Strategy #2: Vision Boards.

To be a well-rounded coach, we have to recognize that the people we work with learn in different ways. Vision boards are a strategy you can use to help visual learners create an image of success.

A vision board is simply a collection of images, quotes, and words that will motivate and help keep you committed to accomplishing your goals. Place your vision board where you will see it every day.

This will keep your goals in the front of your mind and motivate you to achieve them on a daily basis. I keep my vision board above my desk and on my phone and I look at it multiple times each week. It serves as a reminder for me to constantly ask myself: **Is what I am working on right now helping me get to where I want to go?**

The vision board is great for getting your athletes to constantly check in on their progress and refocus on what they want to accomplish.

Strategy #3: Find Their "Why."

Most coaches recognize the importance of goal setting and make some effort to help their athletes with this. But often, I hear frustrations arise when it doesn't seem to be doing a whole lot of good. Despite setting goals, athletes still struggle, lose steam, and give up.

The problem is that **many of the traditional methods of setting goals are too surface-level and fail to recognize the different kinds of deeper motivation and commitment.**

We have our athletes write down their goals, which usually comes out to something like: *"I want to get stronger and add 3 inches to my vertical."*

This can be tricky, because it's not that these are bad goals, but if we stop here, we're not digging deep enough. Saying you want to *"get stronger"* or *"add 3 inches to my vertical"* may be a good starting point, but it won't cut deep enough when things get hard

191

and they want to give up.

We have to do a better job of tying this into a "why" that really connects with the individual on a deep and personal level.

If you are working with someone who continually struggles to bring focus, energy, and commitment to the table, you can help them identify *why they are pursuing their goals on a deeper level.*

I call it "Finding your WHY," and it's proven to be a powerful tool for athletes who've struggled with motivation.

Here's your assignment this week: Take a few minutes to assess your overall game plan for helping your athletes with motivation. Are you encouraging them to get a daily dose of motivation while also providing some ongoing, higher level strategies for sustained focus and commitment?

Try out one of the strategies covered today with one of your athletes this week. Each of the strategies have unique benefits, and while there isn't a wrong answer in terms of which one you use, there may be a better choice based on your specific situation. If you're working with someone who seems to get overwhelmed by the big picture, use the telescope + microscope goal setting strategy to connect how their actions today directly lead to that long-term "someday" goal. If you've tried traditional "write it down" goal setting and it hasn't worked well, the Vision Board strategy is a great option.

Finally, if you have someone who struggles to bring energy and focus and have that "spark," the Finding Your WHY exercise may be just what they need to turn things around.

Brian Cain www.briancain.com

57. Four Areas to Address to Help Athletes Break Out of Slumps

The causes of performance slumps can be grouped into four general categories. First, perhaps the most common cause of slumps is a physical problem. These difficulties include fatigue, minor injuries, and lingering illness. Second, slumps may be due to subtle changes in technique that occur during the course of a season. These changes may be in the execution of the skill or in the timing of the movement. Third, slumps may begin with changes in an athlete's equipment, e.g., loosening of string tension on a tennis racquet or a different weight of a new baseball bat. Particularly in those sports that require elaborate equipment, there is a precise balance between equipment and technique. As a result, a slight change in equipment may alter technique, thereby hurting performance. Fourth, slumps can be caused by psychological factors. Furthermore, the mental contributors may be related to or independent of the athletic involvement. For example, a particularly poor performance may reduce confidence and increase anxiety, which could lead to a prolonged drop in performance. In contrast, issues away from competition such as family difficulties, financial problems, and school struggles may distract concentration, increase stress, and decrease motivation, thus resulting in a performance decline.

Recommendations for Preventing Slumps:
The best way to deal with slumps is to prevent them from happen-

ing. Slumps can be prevented by paying careful attention to the causes of slumps and taking steps to avoid those causes.

Physical. As discussed above, many slumps begin with physical difficulties. More specifically, slumps are often caused by the normal physical wear and tear of the competitive season. As a result, performance slumps may be prevented by paying attention to various factors that influence an athlete's physical state.

One important area that can be addressed is physical condition. Quite simply, athletes who are well-conditioned will be less susceptible to fatigue, injury, and illness. Consequently, a rigorous off-season physical training program and a competitive season physical maintenance program will help minimize slumps due to physical breakdown. Second, a significant part of slump prevention is rest. In other words, physical deterioration can be lessened by actively incorporating rest into athletes' training and competitive regimens. Adequate rest can be assured in several ways. Days off can be built into the weekly training schedule. For example, in sports with weekend competitions, having mandatory Mondays off is a good way to ensure that athletes are able to recover from the prior week's training and the stresses of the previous days' competition.

Third, athletes can reduce the quantity and increase the quality of training as the season progresses. This approach will allow athletes to maintain a high level of health and energy right through the end of the season. This is especially important in sports that have lengthy seasons such as baseball, tennis, and golf.

Fourth, planning a responsible competition schedule can also prevent slumps. Perhaps the most demanding aspect of sports involvement is the actual competition. Competing in too many events is both physically and mentally draining and may be counterproductive for the athlete. As a result, athletes and coaches need to select the competitions that are most important for the athletes and to avoid scheduling events that serve no specified purpose in the athlete's seasonal competitive plan.

Fifth, scheduling time off about three weeks before an important competition, particularly when it is towards the end of the season, can help to ensure a high level of performance. This strategy allows athletes to recover from previous competitions, overcome nagging injuries and illness, focus attention on the upcoming competition, and prepare for the final push toward that competition. Most fundamentally, the best way to reduce the likelihood of a slump due to physical causes is for athletes to listen to their bodies. They need to acknowledge fatigue, injury, and illness and when any are evident, they should be dealt with immediately. Simply put, athletes must learn to work hard and rest hard.

Technical. Slumps that are caused by technical changes can also be prevented by taking steps to maintain sound technique which results in strong performance. First, technique is best developed during the off-season when the primary focus is on technical improvement and there is adequate time to fully acquire the skills. As a result, technically induced performance slumps may be prevented by minimizing technical work done during the competitive season. Working on technique may not only disturb the technique that is producing good performance, it may also hurt performance by reducing confidence and distracting concentration. In addition, maintaining a video library of good technique and performances can be used by athletes and coaches to remind them of proper technique and to compare current with past technique.

Technological. The best way to prevent technologically-related performance slumps is to maintain equipment at its high performance level. For example, if a favorite baseball bat is broken, it should be replaced by another of identical weight and balance.

Psychological. Performance slumps that are caused by psychological factors can be addressed at two levels. First, for those difficulties that arise directly from competition, it is important to have athletes engaged in a regular mental training program. This approach will develop athletes' mental skills in areas such as self-confidence, anxiety, concentration, and motivation, thereby making them more resilient to the negative psychological effects of periodic poor performance. In addition, following poor performance, it is necessary for athletes to actively combat these negative psychological effects by employing these mental skills. This will prevent them from getting caught in a self-perpetuating vicious cycle of low self-confidence and poor performance.

Second, for those difficulties that occur away from the sport, it is necessary for athletes to work them out quickly and effectively. In addition, the previously-learned mental skills can be used to leave these difficulties off the field, so that, at least during competition, athletes are able to maintain their proper focus and intensity, thus preventing a drop in performance.

Jim Taylor, Ph.D www.drjimtaylor.com

58. Six Ways to Come Through in the Clutch

This chapter is addressed directly to athletes.

The biggest secret to you playing your best when it counts the most is learning how to keep yourself CALM and COMPOSED. If you allow yourself to get too nervous or too excited right before or during a competition, then your muscles will tighten up, you'll lose your confidence and your play will suffer. You'll get so nervous that you end up performing tight and tentatively — a mere shadow of your normal self!

Runaway, pre-game nervousness can come from a lot of different sources: how good your opponents are; how big and aggressive they are; how important a competition is; how big the crowd is (and who in it is watching you); whether you'll play well today and win; how "excited" your coach may get; how much playing time you'll get; the court, field or arena you're playing in; whether their team will win or lose; what people may think or say about them, etc.

While there are many things about your competitions that can potentially make you nervous, the true cause of your performance-disrupting nervousness isn't any of the things that I've just mentioned above. The real cause of your out of control nerves is you. It's what's happening INSIDE that is the real cause of stress!

It's not the size, skill level or reputation of your opponents that makes you nervous. It's what you say to yourself about them in the days, hours and minutes leading up to the game, match or race that's the real culprit in sending your heart rate and blood pressure through the roof! Nervousness is always caused by our inner response to the things that are going on outside of us. But here's the good news about that: If you make yourself nervous, then you have the ability to change your inner response to calm yourself down under competitive pressure. Most players who get too nervous to play well do so because of what they focus on and think about as the game approaches.

Focusing on any or all of these things will guarantee that your stress level will go through the attic and your play will get stuck in the cellar! To stay calm under pressure, you must learn to go into competitions with a completely different headset and focus. A championship game plan is a series of little mental goals that you want to bring into the performance with you. If you follow this game plan, it will guarantee that you'll stay calm and relaxed when you perform. Remember, playing your best when it counts the most is all about being loose right before and during your competitions.

#1. *KEEP YOUR CONCENTRATION IN THE "NOW."* When athletes allow their focus of concentration to jump ahead to the future, or drift back to the past, the result is always an increase in their nervousness. If you want to stay cool and calm in the clutch, then you have to train yourself to keep your focus in the NOW — especially during your games, matches or races! This means that leading up to the performance, you don't want to think about and focus on the upcoming opponent and its importance If you want to play loose and relaxed, you must learn to keep your concentration in the now. When you're in the action, you want to focus on one present moment play at a time.

#2. RECOGNIZE WHEN YOUR FOCUS "TIME TRAVELS" AND BRING YOURSELF BACK. It's very easy to understand that you need to focus in the now, but much harder to consistently do it! The way that you stay in the now is by immediately becoming aware whenever your focus drifts back to the past or ahead to the future, then quickly return your concentration to the now. Losing your focus won't make you nervous. What will make you nervous is losing your focus and not bringing it back right away! It's the break in concentration that you don't immediately catch that will drive your stress level through the roof and sabotage your play.

#3. KEEP YOUR FOCUS ON YOU, YOUR JOB AND YOUR PLAY. Allowing your focus to drift to anyone or anything other than you, (i.e. your opponents, who's watching, who might be disappointed in you, how well your teammates may be playing, what the coach is thinking, etc.) will quickly make you feel nervous. Staying focused on you and your job will keep you calm and confident. This also means that whenever you perform, you want to make sure that you don't compare yourself to others. Comparison will always make you too nervous to play at your best.

#4. LEAVE YOUR OUTCOME GOALS AT HOME. One of the biggest tension-inducing mental mistakes that you can make as an athlete is to take your goals with you into the competition. For example, you think, "I want to go 3 for 4," "pitch a shutout," "win this tournament," "score a goal," "break two minutes," or "prove to the coaches that I'm good." Focusing on such outcome goals will make you too nervous to play well. Instead, leave your goals at home and keep your focus in the action, on "this" play, shot, pitch or move, one moment at a time!

#5. *KEEP YOUR MIND DISTRACTED BEFORE AND AFTER GAMES*. Thinking gets most athletes into trouble and makes them nervous. While you can't really stop yourself from thinking, you can purposely distract yourself from it. So, in the days and minutes leading up to a big performance or tournament, keep busy. Do not allow yourself a lot of free time to think. Focus on your homework, read a book, watch a movie, listen to music, get involved in non-sports related conversations with friends and do things to keep yourself busy and distracted. "Changing the channel" in this way will help you stay calm and composed in the days and hours leading up to your BIG performances.

#6. *KEEP YOUR FOCUS OF CONCENTRATION AWAY FROM THE "UNCONTROLLABLES."*
There are a lot of things that happen in your sport that you do not have direct control over. Any time an athlete focuses on an "uncontrollable" (UC), he or she will get really nervous, lose their confidence and play badly. Make a list of all of the things about this upcoming competition that you can't directly control. For example, the officiating; the crowd; coaching decisions, (i.e. playing time); the future, such as the outcome of the game, how well you'll play, winning or losing; how you are feeling that day; other people's expectations; etc., and post the list in a highly visible place in your room. Keep in mind that these UCs are mental traps. They are lying in wait for you and every other athlete in that competition. The only way to avoid a trap is to know that it is there.

Alan Goldberg, Ed.D. www.competitivedge.com

The best athletes have the ability to discipline themselves to eliminate everything except what they are trying to accomplish.

DALE BROWN

SECTION VI

Best Team Building and Leadership Strategies

59. Seven Question Team Building Exercise

Here are seven questions that teams can discuss in the preseason to help them bond together.

1) What do I do to help us all work well together as a team?

2) What do my teammates do to help us work well together as a team?

3) What are all the things we did in a peak game that helped us work well together?

4) What could we do create team unity and cohesiveness that we're not already doing?

5) What do we need to do to improve as a team and to be more successful?

6) What can I do personally to encourage and support my teammates?

7) I think important team goals for our team should be ...

a.

b.

c.

d.

e.

60. Four Common Team Captain Mistakes

You want your team captains to be like extensions of your coaching on the floor. But some players don't always lead in a way that helps rise the play of everyone around them. Here are 4 mistakes that you should watch out for so your captains don't make them.

1) *Thinking they know everything.* A good captain will ask a teammate for their input before trying to force anything on them.

2) *Learn to differentiate between different and wrong.* Two players may each get positive results, but they may arrive there using different approaches. If a team captain starts to make all other players "do it exactly like I do," they will alienate rather than motivate their teammates.

3) *Not taking time to get to know their teammates.* If they don't understand at least somewhat what drives their teammates, they will struggle in their role as captain.

4) *Ignoring problems and not taking responsibility.* If a captain sees a teammate who isn't doing what they should be – on or off the court – and says or does nothing, they aren't doing their job. Team leaders are responsible for everything that happens in their group. What other players do or fail to do reflects on the captain. They have to step up as a captain and confront issues as they arise.

61. Top Ten Responsibilities of a Team Captain

1) *Team Organization* – With the busy schedules of student-athletes, captains remind players of commitments and changes in schedules and reinforce team structure.

2) *Team Connections* – Captains are responsible for connecting with their teammates on a daily basis to ensure all players feel like valued members of the team.

3) *Locker Room Climate* – Captains try to keep the locker room talk and banter productive and motivating – win or lose.

4) *Practice Leader* – Captains keep the practice environment productive, energetic and efficient.

5) *Go to Players* – Captains usually want the ball with the game on the line and will make the clutch plays when called upon.

6) *Lead by Example and Vocal* – Captains are the first ones expected to speak up during team meetings. They are the first to go during a drill. They are very familiar with the system and what the coach wants executed and they can effectively communicate that message with their teammates.

7) *Competitive* – Captains are responsible for setting the competitive tone by getting the most out of every drill, rep, practice and game opportunity.

8) *Challenge Teammates* – Ensuring that teammates follow the

competitive tone that they set.

9) *Make Everyone Else Better Around You* – Captains help rein-force coach teachings and strategy instruction. They also help teammates make in-game adjustments.

10) *Improve Overall Team Performance* – Once a game starts, in most sports play on the court is more dictated by players than coaches. Captains must take over a "coach on the court" role during games.

Michael Voight, Ph.D.

62. Coach K: Creating a Respect Culture and Goal Setting Mistakes

On creating respect of players: "The best way to gain respect is to tell them the truth. Look them in the eye and tell them, "This is the way it is." Give it to them straight – both the good and the bad. Not just, "You are not playing hard enough or giving enough effort." But also, "You're good – here is how you can be even better." When you look at a player straight in the eye and tell him the truth over and over – that's the basis of your relationship. You develop the best of relationships because it's founded on trust. That's the key building block to future success.

On setting goals, including specific number of wins: "I've never set goals in terms of wins and losses. I've always talked to my players about the possibility of winning a championship. The reason I don't do the wins and losses is that I want the mental approach that every game is winnable. If you set a goal for say 20 wins and making the

NCAA tournament, I think the danger is that certain sense of satisfaction creeps in that can prevent you from going farther. Then you'd be stopping yourself. On the other hand, what if you have a few key injuries on a team capable of winning more than 20. That same team may win 17, but that was still a solid achievement based on what they were dealing with. I would rather define success for my team rather than have specific wins and losses define us."

63. Wooden's Seven Leadership Principles

In *The Essential Wooden*, Coach John Wooden summarized his leadership philosophies. Here are seven keys from his book.

1. **Operate with a sense of urgency.** This is summed up with a famous phrase that Wooden coined: "Live as though you may die tomorrow. Learn as though you will live forever."

Wooden says that at the heart of every effective leader is the idea of seeking knowledge with a sense of urgency.

2. **Build trust with your team as quickly as possible.** "Without trust between the team and the leader, there is really no team at all – just a collection of individuals who don't amount to much." Wooden says that the star of any team is the team itself rather than any one individual.

3. **Apply the four rules of learning:** *explanation, demonstration, imitation, and repetition.*

4. **Whatever values, attitudes, and ideals a manager or coach wants a team to embrace are best accomplished by adopting them him - or herself.**

"Be hardest on yourself – the model for what you want your team to become. Don't look for others to be your quality control expert."

5. **Stay hungry.** A little success can be dangerous. "If you are content when you reach a goal or important milestone, you can lose the desire to keep improving. You will fall into the trap of thinking that past success will occur in the future without even greater effort."

6. **Constantly ask the team for complete commitment and effort – then accept the blame when the team falters.**

7. **Put the good of the team first – consider yourself part of the team instead of above it.**

64. Three Steps to Energize the Team Mission

After you have developed a team mission statement, it's time to make sure your team has a well-defined mission as well. Mission statements are best prepared in the off-season and can be adjusted slightly during the season depending on circumstances.

Recommendation: Part of your job is to get athletes to buy into the vision you have for the team. Here are some guidelines to consider to reinvigorate your team mission statement.

1) **Make sure your mission makes sense.** Did you go winless last year? Then a mission to win a conference or national title is a mission that doesn't make sense for the current squad.

Brainstorm with your team to come up with a mission statement that is challenging, yet attainable. Create a list of action steps you need to achieve your mission.

Example: A basketball team's mission statement was summed up by a motto they put on their t-shirts: "Find a Way."

Using that motto as a source of inspiration, they outlined some of aspects the team would be known by such as always diving on the floor for a loose ball, winning the rebounding battle, and being in the best shape possible to win the close games down the stretch.

2) **Reinforce the importance of the mission.** In business, organizations will come up with mottoes like "Quality is Our Business." But they don't make any effort to sell their staff on the concept. As a coach, you need to constantly go back and remind your team what their mission is. This is something that can't be repeated enough. A daily reminder to say "Find a Way," or whatever your team slogan, is a great way to end practice.

3) **Bring your mission statement to life.** Posters with the mission statement and top goals listed are a good thing to have placed in your locker room. But an even better way to reinforce your mission is to have call out players who have exhibited (either at practice or during games) the winning traits that connect with your mission at team meetings. Take a little extra time to celebrate positive role

models that the rest of the team can pattern in their actions. These don't have to be starters or stars. The more you celebrate those who exemplify the team mission, the more willing practitioners you'll have.

65. Wooden's 18 Character Qualities for Coaches

1. Attentiveness to Detail. You must prepare to win in order to be a winner. Failure to prepare is preparing to fail.

2. Impartiality. This is a must, but you must remember that you must not treat everyone alike as they are all different. Give each one the treatment earned and deserved.

3. Teaching Skill. It isn't enough that you know the game, you must be able to teach it. Follow the laws of learning.

4. Discipline. Most essential for proper concentration and group organization.

5. Affability. The coach must be of an affable disposition because of the various groups with whom he must associate.

6. Forcefulness. You must be firm without being bullheaded.

7. Alertness. Constant observation of all things going on around you is necessary for improved learning and decision making.

8. Optimism. The pessimist isn't likely to produce a confident team that will play near to their full capability.

9. Desire to Improve. Lack of ambition will result in complacency and laziness.

10. Vision. A picture of the possible must be shown to your players to provide a goal for them.

11. Consideration For Others. You must be truly considerate of others if you expect them to be considerate of you. You must listen to them if you want them to listen to you.

12. Resourcefulness. You must be ever ready to make necessary adjustments according to the situation and the personnel that you have available.

13. Cooperativeness. An essential for all who work with others and are dependent on others in various ways.

13. Leadership. Trust be commanded, not demanded. Others are working with you, not for you. Be interested in finding the best way rather than having your own way.

14. Industriousness. There is no substitute for work. Worthwhile things should never be easy to attain.

15. Enthusiasm. If you are to stimulate others, your heart must be in your work. Enthusiasm brushes off upon those with whom you come in contact.

16. Sympathy. You must be truly interested in those under your supervision and be sympathetic with their problems.

17. Self-control. Good judgment must be exercised in your decisions and they must be made through reason not emotion.

18. Sincerity. Insincerity can be spotted very quickly and cause loss of respect.

Excerpted from website: CoachingToolBox.net

66. Golden State Team Building Dinners

Golden State Warriors basketball team does something unheard of in the NBA: They eat together. "In the 26 years I've been in the league," said associate head coach Alvin Gentry, "I find it to be very rare."

The Warriors are the outlier NBA team that actually goes out to dinner on the road. Instead of trekking off on their own — like most players, especially on losing teams — the Warriors make a habit out of huge team meals. It isn't unusual for their team outings to draw 10 players or more.

It is an uncommon example of a professional sports team bonding like Little Leaguers, and helps explain why this team is widely considered one of the most close-knit. "Chemistry is not something you can fake," Warriors forward David Lee said. "You either have it or you don't."

Despite their paychecks and their fame, NBA players try to escape their jobs on the road, just like anyone else on a business trip. When players have free time, they tend to stick to themselves or hang out in cliques.

Most players on off days are "stray bullets," Warriors center Andrew Bogut said, arriving at the team hotel and not seeing each other until their light pregame practice the next morning. "That's just the norm in the NBA," said Bogut. "We go out together and eat together way more than any other team I've been on."

Golden State's unusual technique for team bonding wasn't one of Head Coach Steve Kerr's masterstrokes. At no point this season did his staff suggest anything like this, Gentry said. The players say there is a much simpler reason for their team dinners: They just like being around each other. That camaraderie shows on the court. It is especially apparent when the Warriors hit the road. Like most young professionals, players decide when and where to eat with a team-wide group text message.

Players say that this kinship matters more than ever. One of the spoils of winning is that successful teams tend to stay intact, said Lee, and that continuity can make good teams even better. "I think there was probably a time in sports when you could put a bunch of jerks together and they'd find a way to win, but not now," he said.

When the team returns from summer break, we have an exercise called Show and Tell. Each player has to bring something from home that is important to her, usually something no one else knows about. Before each practice, a different player takes five minutes to do their speech. This brings the team closer together.

GAIL GOESTENKORS

67. Develop Loyalty on a Coaching Staff

Talk with coaches and they say that what they want most in their professional relationships is loyalty. With good reason, winning staffs appear to be bound by loyalty, while losing staffs seem to be void of it. The technical definitions of loyalty according to the Oxford dictionary are trustworthiness and dependability. In the practical environment of coaching, loyalty can be described more specifically.

Recommendation: Here are some practical suggestions to help you develop loyalty amongst your coaching staff. Three perspectives (supervisory, peer, and subordinates) are addressed that cover the expectations of each role.

1) Supervisory suggestions: • Talk with subordinates honestly and candidly regarding their performance. There is no greater form of respect than candid honesty. • Give your subordinates as much respect as you give to your boss. • Listen without interruption or judgment to compliments and criticisms. Anyone on staff who demonstrates their passion by volunteering criticism should be heard. • Demonstrate as much commitment to your subordinate's success as to your boss's. • Acknowledge the work of your subordinates and share staff recognition. Recognition from a superior is a powerful motivator. • Teach subordinates when they do things incorrectly — don't criticize them personally. Critique the performance critically, and you challenge the subordinate — criticize the performer, and expect mutiny.

2) Peer suggestions: • Give options on all issues — whether they're in your assigned area or not. This is what's commonly referred to as teamwork. • Contribute to each other's success unselfishly. • Be thick-skinned enough to take input from others, thus putting your personal insecurities to the side when dealing with professional issues. • Listen to each other without interruption or personal judgment. • Cover for each other's weaknesses — don't complain about them. • Share a positive rivalry. Embrace competition within the working environment but be each other's greatest fan along the way.

3) Subordinate suggestions: • Follow directions as they're given. Your ability to follow directions will have a direct correlation to your success. • Do more than your job description requires.
• Candidly share disagreements and criticisms — listen to and support your bosses' final decisions completely. • Support silently or verbally all of your bosses' decisions. • Serve as messengers and translators who explain to players the head coach's decision and rationale. • Listen to the boss without interruption or personal judgment. • Cover the bosses' weaknesses, don't complain about them.

Conclusion: Team success can not be realized without staff loyalty. Follow the previous suggestions and you'll have staff unity and team success.

Tim Wakeman, M.S. College Strength Coach

68. Golden State Uses Humor to Bond

NBA champion Golden State were a super team. They were villains — Supervillains.

Coach Steve Kerr wasn't insulted. He was inspired. The Warriors' coach thought it had comedic potential. So when Golden State's players came to training camp, Kerr made sure there were presents in their lockers: their very own "Supervillains" shirts.

His players got the joke. Then they got in on the joke. The Warriors soon posed for an informal team photo at Stephen Curry's home underneath letter-shaped balloons that spelled out "Supervillains." There was even a customized Snapchat filter. They had turned the put-down into a punchline. "We're always in search of something funny," said Golden State assistant coach Bruce Fraser.

The Warriors were loose because they won, but they also won because they were loose.

Sports teams packed with highly paid professional athletes and their egos can be notoriously difficult to manage.

Before one of the Final games, Kerr greeted his team with a locker room message reading: "I want you to go out there and play with great joy. That's who we are."

The team's humor, like their offense, was egalitarian. Zaza Pachulia decided that outscoring Klay Thompson in a playoff game was a historic occasion worthy of commemoration. He framed a copy of a fake San Francisco Chronicle front page with the headline: "HELL FREEZES OVER: Pachulia outscores Thompson."

The Warriors used comedy all season to keep rolling and even to deflate the few bad moments. After the only losing streak of the season, for example, the song they blasted at practice was Bobby McFerrin's "Don't Worry, Be Happy."

"The humor comes from what happens within our daily lives," Fraser said. "We don't have a writer's room. It's not like we've got guys in the back working on humor instead of analytics."

The Warriors' embrace of comedy is surprisingly crucial to their success. It's the foundation of their office culture in a workplace where the office is everywhere: the locker room, film room, weight room, team plane, team hotel, team bus and, of course, the basketball court.

One way to think about professional basketball players is as co-workers who spend all their time together. They might have hated each other if the Warriors didn't have a way of diffusing such tension: laughing at it. Scholars have found that employees in funnier business environments are better at their jobs and happier when they're in the office.

A study published by the *Journal of Managerial Psychology* showed humor positively correlates with work performance. "One conclusion derived from these findings," the paper says, "might be that organizations should attempt to cultivate humor within the workplace."

69. 20 Tips for Leading Generation Z

The following chapter on leading Millennials and Generation Z was excerpted from the Church Sports Outreach blog. While the principles are more directed to the workplace, many of the same concepts can apply to your athletic teams as well.

1. Give them freedom with their schedule. Even limited freedom to vote when they practice will help build team trust and motivation.

2. Provide them projects, not a career. Career is just not the same anymore. They desire options.

3. Create a family environment. Work, family and social are all intertwined, so make sure the work environment is experiential and family oriented. Everything is connected.

4. Cause is important. Tie in compassion and justice to the "normal." Causes and opportunities to give back are important.

5. Embrace social media. It's here to stay. (See 6).

6. They are more tech savvy than any other generation ever. Technology is the norm. Xbox, iPhones, laptops, iPads are just normal. If you want a response, text first, then call. Or send a Facebook or Instagram message.

7. Lead each person uniquely. Customize your approach.

8. Make authenticity and honesty the standard for your corporate

culture. Millennials are cynical at their core, and don't trust someone just because they are in charge.

9. Millennials are not as interested in "climbing the corporate lad-
der." But instead more concerned about making a difference and
leaving their mark.

10. Give them opportunities early with major responsibility. They
don't want to wait their turn. They want to make a difference now.
And will find an outlet for influence and responsibility somewhere
else if you don't give it to them. Empower them early and often.

11. All about the larger win, not the personal small gain. Young
leaders in general have an abundance mentality instead of scarcity
mentality.

12. Partnering and collaboration are important. Not interested in
drawing lines. Collaboration is the new currency, along with gen-
erosity.

13. Not about working for a personality. Not interested in laboring
long hours to build a temporal kingdom for one person. But will
work their guts out for a cause and vision bigger than themselves.

14. Deeply desire mentoring, learning and discipleship. Many older
leaders think Millennials aren't interested in generational wisdom
transfer. Not true at all. Younger leaders are hungry for mentoring
and discipleship, so build it into your organizational environment.

15. Coach them and encourage them. They want to gain wisdom

through experience. Come alongside them don't just tell them what to do.

16. Create opportunities for quality time — individually and corporately. They want to be led by example, and not just by words.

17. Hold them accountable. They want to be held accountable by those who are living it out. Measure them and give them constant feedback.

18. They've been exposed to just about everything, so the sky is the limit in their minds. Older leaders have to understand younger leaders have a much broader and global perspective, which makes wowing Millennials much more difficult.

19. Recognize their values, not just their strengths. It isn't just about the skills they bring to the team. Don't use them without truly knowing them.

20. Provide a system that creates stability. Clear expectations with the freedom to succeed, and providing stability on the emotional, financial, and organizational side.

70. Eight Ways to Improve Asst. Coach Performance

Here are eight suggestions that can build staff unity, discipline and create an atmosphere that makes your assistant want to achieve more. No guarantees, but following these suggestions should improve your assistant's practice and game day performance.

1) Loyalty. This is definitely a two-way street. The head coach can demonstrate loyalty in a number of ways. First, always back up your assistants. Don't lay the blame for a mistake or a loss on an assistant. When referring to coaching decisions the head coach should emphasize the "we" concept instead of "I" to promote staff unity. Be willing to spread credit around to an assistant when deserved.

Above all, the head coach must do everything in his power to help an assistant advance in the profession regardless of how valuable he is to the program.

2) Delegate Responsibility. Make sure each assistant knows exactly what is expected of him or her, both on and off the field. Outline all responsibilities (practice, administrative, etc.). Be explicit, and don't leave room for doubt or error that could later lead to staff friction.

3) Let the Assistants Do Their Job. Once you have delegated responsibility to the coach you must give them freedom to work. Let them go out and coach their way. Allow leeway — as long as you both agree with the end result.

4) Criticize in Private. Never criticize or correct an assistant in public or in front of the team. When a coach must be corrected it must be done in the privacy of the coaches' office.

5) Be Open. Provide an environment in which an assistant can feel comfortable expressing new ideas. Encourage this atmosphere in your coaches' meetings. Frequently ask for their opinions during planning sessions. Take time to consider their ideas even when they don't agree with your thoughts. Make the assistant explain his idea completely if it may have merit.

6) Make the Best Possible Use of Each Assistant. If at all possible, *let the assistant coach in his area of primary interest.* Make use of whatever special talents they may have.

This may mean that you have to adjust your and your staff's responsibilities into different coaching areas. This may not be practical in all coaching situations, especially when you have a very small staff. But remember **the quickest way for an assistant to lose enthusiasm is to be forced to coach an area in which they have no background or interest.**

7) Keep the Assistant Informed. Share your ideas and thoughts openly with your assistants and help them become better coaches. Remember they are looking for a learning experience. Don't keep any secrets from them. Show confidence in them by sharing all the information you receive about the program (administrative memos, state directives, conference meetings, clinics, etc.). Run off a copy for each assistant. Above all, never surprise a coach in practice with new material that hasn't been discussed before.

8) Evaluate the Assistant. Every coach in your program deserves a formal, written evaluation at the conclusion of each season. Privately sit down and discuss the assistant's strong and weak points and what changes (if any) will be expected before next season. A copy of this evaluation signed by both the head and assistant coach should be filed with the athletic director or principal.

71. Eight Common Leadership Communication Mistakes

1) *Passing Judgment Too Quickly.* Try this: For one week, treat every idea that comes from another person in your organization with complete neutrality. Don't take sides. Don't even verbally express an opinion. If you think the idea has no merit, simply reply with a comment like, "Thanks, I hadn't considered that." Or "Thanks, you've given me something to think about." This sort of neutral response will soon be part of your vocabulary. You will reduce arguments with staff. Co-workers will see you as having a more open mind to their input.

2) *Making Destructive Comments.* Sarcastic remarks may some-times be an effective motivator to players and staff, but too many erode team cohesion over time. One of the greatest errors leaders make is to bring up a past mistake that is forgotten by everyone but you. If you have a habit of saying things like, "Do you remember the time you… (fill in blank with past error)?" before speaking, ask yourself, "Will what I am about to say help our team?" or "Will this comment help the person I'm talking to or about?"

3) *Starting with "No," "But" or "However."* When you start a sen-tence with either of these words, no matter how friendly the tone, the message the other person gets is "You are wrong!" For example, when you start a sentence with "Yes, but …" the other person knows they are going to be contradicted.

4) *Withholding Information.* We now live and work in the informa-tion age. Intentionally withholding information is the opposite of adding value. Reflect on how you might react if any of the follow-

ing events occurred: • You were not copied on an email sent to parents' recruits. • A moment when you felt like you were the last to learn about something.

Not sharing information rarely achieves the desired effect. To lead more effectively, you need to inspire loyalty rather than suspicion. Sometimes withholding information can be accidental such as forgetting to include someone in your discussions or meetings or delegating a task to an assistant without taking the time to show how you want the task done.

5) *Failing to Give Proper Recognition.* If you don't recognize another person's contribution to a team's success, you not only sow the seeds of staff dissent, you deprive the person the emotional payoff that comes hearing that their contribution mattered. They will feel ignored.

6) *Playing Favorites.* We have to be careful not to end up treating people like the pets who heap unconditional admiration on us. The net result is that you encourage behavior that serves you, but is not necessarily in the best interest of the team. If everyone is just trying to get in your good graces, the real work that needs to be done can get neglected.

7) *Punishing the Messenger.* No one enjoys hearing bad news, but if you want honesty in the workplace, your staff needs to feel free to speak up about weak areas without getting hammered. Asking "What went wrong and how do we fix it?" should be part of your open dialogue.

8) *Passing the Buck.* A leader who can't shoulder blame is not someone who will build a staff/team who will follow him or her into battle. Passing the buck is the dark flip side of claiming credit that others deserve. Instead of depriving others of their role in team success, you blame them with the shame of team failure.

72. How College Basketball Programs Build Team Trust

When men's college basketball coaches navigate the maze of friends, family members and third-party influences who can drive wedges between them and their players, one thing becomes painfully clear.

"Trust is everything," said college coach Archie Miller.

It's also hard to come by. According to the Study of Student-Athlete Social Environments, Division I men's basketball players are less trusting of coaches than male athletes in any other college sport. When responding to the survey statement:

"My coaches can be trusted," 53% of Division I men's basketball players said they agreed or strongly agreed. Other sports only faired slightly better with wrestling coaches topping the most trusted at 78 percent followed by track/cross country (68%), swimming and hockey (each 63%). Football was 59%.

In each of the other statements — "Most people can be trusted," "I trust my teammates as much as anybody in my life" and "My team-mates have my back regardless of the situation" — men's basketball players had the lowest levels of agreement of any men's sport.

Generation Z (born after 2000) have low levels of trust, significantly lower than other generations. In the Pew survey, 19% agreed that most people can be trusted. "That number is incredibly low, and there's some sense that it's not only because of their age — younger people tend to be more cynical in general — but also that this young generation is really cynical," one researcher said. "That's what happens with a low level of trust."

Trust is built between a player and coach on a case-by-case basis, so it can be difficult to decipher why trust numbers are lower in basketball across the board. One factor that erodes player-coach relationships is annual coaching turnover. That in turn can partly account for the high rate of transfers.

Perhaps an even more simplistic way of looking at the trust issue is this: If expectations do not match reality, the bond of trust may break. Or, at the very least, the athlete will perceive that it's broken. "Trust is probably low because expectations are unrealistic," college coach Jay Wright said. "Everybody expects things to happen so quickly. There are so many variables, like an injury or a player returning after saying he was going to leave early — and he's at your position. All those variables change what the player's perception of what his freshman year was supposed to be. A lot of times, it comes down to your freshman year."

It's one thing for a coach to promise a player that he'll play at a certain position or for a certain amount of minutes per game, and for those promises to be broken. As Miller put it, "You've got to be what you say, and say what you mean. They're going to call B.S. on you the first time it doesn't look right."

The coaches interviewed for this story said they aim to paint a realistic picture and make sure not to make promises they could possibly break. They feel they provide an opportunity for their players to compete for a spot and work hard to get minutes — and there are no guarantees.

Still, sometimes the concept of earning playing time and earning trust get confused.

"When a player's not playing, a lot of time the player will say, 'The coach doesn't trust me. He's not playing me,'" college and NBA coach Billy Donovan said. "The coach may not trust him on the floor in certain situations, but that's totally different than, 'Do you trust my word? Do you trust what I'm saying? Have I lied to you?' "There is a difference between a coach not trusting a player in a game because he may not be experienced enough or is making mistakes, from a coach saying something and not following through with his word. (You have to) get a player to understand the difference."

Donovan says communication is the way to offset any differences between a player's and coach's expectations, and that talking can help explain a coach's decision to play/not play someone. He, like many of his peers, tries to build lasting relationships with players off the court.

"Trust in general, particularly with kids who come from backgrounds that may not foster a lot of trust, is a challenge," college coach Shaka Smart said. "We have four guys on our team that had fathers in their homes growing up; we have mostly guys who are not used to trusting a male figure in their life. There's no magic formula. I think (what helps build trust is) spending time off the court, letting these guys know we care about them beyond just the basketball floor, being hard on them."

Ways to build trust: A lot of times, unrealistic expectations — and the problems that follow — stem from the recruiting process.

It's a peculiar system, one where coaches try to impress players as players try to impress coaches. But instead of fawning over teenagers and making promises, coaches are learning that the best way to approach recruiting is with honesty.

"You can't tell guys they're going to be your best player, that it's going to be easy, you come here I'm going to make you a star," college coach Mick Cronin said. "We don't tell guys that. (We say,) 'We're going to love you, coach you, try to help you grow up. I'm going to try to motivate you to do your best every day and teach you, coach you as best I can. I can't make you a star.'

"You can't mislead people because then the relationship is doomed to fail before they even get to campus, because it's unrealistic." Jay Wright said sometimes he errs on the side of negativity — or reality — instead of espousing all the benefits of joining his program.

"We say to the guys, 'We're hoping what we're telling you right now may not be as attractive as you want it to be, but you realize when we're coaching you, you realize it's the truth.' It allows us to coach them."

73. Building a Culture of Team Leadership with Good Captains

This chapter features an interview with sports leadership expert Jeff Janssen on various aspects of team leadership. Janssen has pioneered the Team Leadership Academy, which began at the University of North Carolina.

After you have identified the group called "rising stars," the soph- omores and juniors who display high leadership potential, what are some of the methods you teach to increase their leadership capabil- ities?

Early on, we have them assess where they are right now as leaders. I have them answer 24 questions that explore their abilities as a vocal leader and a leader by example. This exercise helps them identify where their two strengths are and what two areas they need to improve on. It all starts with the question, 'Are you leading your- self effectively?' The only way you are ever going to gain the trust, credibility and respect of your teammates and coaches is to 'walk your own talk.'

The early part of leadership development focuses on making the athlete ask themselves hard questions like, 'Are you displaying in your behavior and attitude the kind of leadership skills we need to have?'

Besides modeling good behavior themselves, what else can a student leader do to positively impact his or her team and become an agent of change?

A lot of leadership involves creating a vision for the group. Then they need to create a sense of hope among other players that we can make this vision a reality.

This can be very difficult, especially with teams that don't have a great winning tradition. One of the things we want to do with leaders is develop a 'critical mass.' There are probably several players on the team who are feeling the same frustration with where the team is that the leaders do. It's the job of the team leader to reach out and find a core group of people who want to change the status quo. It's the leader's job to give them a plan and a way to do that.

Finding the ring leaders within the various subgroups and start to develop a working relationship with them is key. Subgroup examples include those that just hang out and socialize together. At the college level, it could be the various classes – freshman, sophomores, etc.

Once you get the leaders of the subgroups on board with the plan, a bunch of other dominos will fall the way you want them to. It's a process that involves constant evaluation. To create that vision, team leaders must ask questions like: "Who do I have on board with the program? Who do I need to get on board? What must be done to get people excited about the vision we have developed? What is our concrete plan we can work on together on the short term basis to get things moving in the right direction?"

*Let's say you have a situation where a student athlete wants to take
a more active leadership role but coaches and/or teammates don't
think this person is right for that role. Any advice on how to diffuse
this potentially volatile situation?*

First, you have to really talk to this player about what it takes to be
a leader. There are so many facets to leadership that not everyone
is a fit for that role. Going back to the 24 question leadership evaluation, I'll have the team leaders take the test, and then ask coaches
and teammates to evaluate the leaders using the same questions.

One of the questions asks if they are one of the hardest workers on
the team. On a 1 to 5 scale, they evaluate themselves and then they
get evaluated by teammates and coaches.

Often a player may be confused as to why they aren't respected as
a leader and not voted as a captain. In some cases, I will show them
their average rating by teammates and coaches. Obviously, I don't
share any specific comments that were made, but they can see the
average total.

For example, "You give yourself a 5 on question six about work
ethic, but the team and coaches rate you a 2.5." This can be a harsh
wake up call. But it is better and more compassionate to tell the
person on the front end that there are areas they need to develop
before they can be a team leader rather than letting them hang in
limbo for a year.

Often times, you have one or two players who speak up and are
very vocal at team meetings, yet have very little respect from their

teammates. It's better to be told in a private setting away from other players that they have some areas they need to work on first, so they don't dig a further hole for themselves in terms of respect and credibility.

With this evaluation, you will often times see players score themselves a 115 out of 120 total points. Then you will see the coaching staff rate him or her at an 87 and teammates even a few points lower. The truth may hurt initially, but it gives the kid a chance to go back and look at what it takes to lead him or herself.

By giving them feedback in a private setting, they can see exactly what areas they need to focus on to gain respect from teammates. It helps clarify the frustration they might be feeling of why they don't have the respect of teammates.

It also hopefully lets them know that they shouldn't be as vocal if they have some areas they need to work on themselves. It helps from a team building stand point as well, since these players won't try to assert themselves as a leader when they shouldn't because they don't have a leadership platform to stand on.

We know how important it is to groom the leaders. But not everyone is cut out for that role. What about the followers?

A lot of kids coming in have a problem with authority – either from a coach or team captain. Getting kids to understand that they need to follow good leadership can be a challenge. I'm playing around with different ways to make this concept sink in. One of the ideas is to have customized sponges, which would be given to freshmen after they enroll. It would be a metaphor to remind them that their job coming into the program is to be a sponge – to soak up the experience of the juniors and seniors who have gone before you and the coaches who have been here a long time. Rather than come in stubborn and hardheaded, come up and be a sponge and they will learn from others experiences, by being respectful and observant.

Older athletes can get frustrated with their younger counterparts especially those coming out of high school with big reputations. They have to know that this is a process that takes time.

The key for the older leaders to understand is that they need the freshman and younger players to have a successful season. Team leaders can't just drop the ball and tune these players out because they don't like how they act. The veteran leaders have to be the bigger person and figure out a way to connect with the younger players.

John Madison, Editor www.championshipperform.com/books

74. Phil Jackson's Team First Philosophy

Professional basketball coach Phil Jackson led teams to 10 NBA titles as a coach, making him the all-time championship leader.

During his tenure with the Chicago Bulls, Jackson used various motivational tactics including surprise field trips in the cities they traveled to, assigning books for the individual player to read based on their personality and interests, and even having a pre-game nap time when he thought the team could use a break in routine.

"I would like to take even more side trips with the players. When we're in Washington, DC, I'd like to take the players to the Senate chamber instead of the shoot around. I'd like to take them to museums or historical monuments. College coaches and business groups can do these sort of things sometimes. It's a terrific team builder."

Attention to the task at hand is one of Jackson's keys to success: "Whether on the court or off, what I call for in my people is full awareness and attention. That's really what Zen is all about, waking up and being mindful. As a team, my players have come to realize that, yes, they've got to have that kind of awareness and, yes, they've got to be extremely alert on the floor. In a sense, they become policemen of themselves, and that's really more fun for a coach to watch happen than anything else," Jackson said.

For Jackson, quality team management is knowing which side of a person to appeal to. He sees it as a choice between materialism and spirituality.

"I like to focus on the spiritual side. Even for people who don't consider themselves spiritual in a religious way, you need to convince them that creating a team is a spiritual act. People have to surrender their own egos, so that the result is bigger than the sum of its parts. A Christian could relate in terms of surrendering their will to God. A Buddhist could relate via the emphasis on having compassion for teammates. I've discovered that approaching problems from a compassionate perspective, trying to empathize with the player and looking at the situation from their point of view is helpful. It can have a transforming effect on the team," he noted.

Jackson believes it's important to create a balance between structure and freedom.

"You need to give your people a foundation so they aren't lost at sea. For instance, our triangle offense puts three players in a particular place on the floor. But you have to make sure everyone has the freedom to act. In this offense, the cuts and passes aren't programmed. You have to know instinctively where everyone else is going to go. This gets everyone involved, and the players end up working like five fingers on a hand."

In Los Angeles he was up to his old tricks — this time with different stars and new challenges. According to Shaq O'Neal: "He kept me on a straight path. I'm the type of person who respects discipline. He really doesn't have to raise his voice to me. Whenever I do something crazy, Phil will just give me a look."

For the late star Kobe Bryant, he had to take a different approach. He harshly criticized Bryant publicly because Bryant strayed from the game plan and almost cost the Lakers a victory. Afterwards, he brought Bryant in for a discussion with Michael Jordan to reinforce the message of team play.

"Michael knew the importance of playing inside a system," Jackson said. "Kobe has great playground instincts, but this is the first time he has had to work within the confines of a system. He bucks against that sometimes. Hearing about the benefits from a legend who has worked effectively within a system was something Kobe needed to hear," Jackson said.

Jackson has been described as an authoritarian who knows when to tighten the reins and when to ease up.

According to former Laker General Manager Jerry West, "The best coaches have a great belief in themselves and in their own unique way get players to buy in. Every successful coach needs an ingredient: the intuitive ability to change a conflict situation into a team building one. Phil has a knack for that."

The days of the 'my way or the high way' are quickly fading into the past. Jackson doesn't believe in the 'controlaholic' style of management that worked for some well known coaches in the past. He prefers a more laid back style that suits his personality.

Sometimes Jackson's low-key approach frustrated his assistant coaches like Tex Winter: "I've never known anyone who handles a crisis the way Phil does. He's able to read the big picture and not let the emotions of the moment take control over him. Things can be going really bad on the court and I'll be screaming at Phil to take a timeout and start earning that huge salary of yours. He'll often turn to me and say, 'Let them work it out themselves.' Many times they do."

His emphasis on the importance of team was summed up in a quote he told the Bulls during one of their championship runs: *"For the strength of the pack is the wolf and the strength of the wolf is the pack."* - Rudyard Kipling.

"Above all, you must contribute your whole self and not just your athletic self. Look at the San Antonio team who won the title a few years ago. Many of the team were involved in a prayer group. There are other belief systems as well. I've used the concept of a tribe. In a tribe, you are a club where all the members help one another. The point is to build mutual respect," Jackson said.

The only way to win consistently is to give everyone — from the stars to the 12th man — a vital role on the team. He believes all team members must grow together.

"The ball is like a microphone or spotlight, the more it's in your hands, the less anybody else has the chance to shine. If you start sharing, others can step up and contribute. If you can't live with that, you'll never win a championship," he said.

For Jackson, quality team management is knowing which side to appeal to. He sees a spiritual side to athletics that others miss.

Things haven't always been rosy for the master team builder. When Michael Jordan had retired and the Bulls were playing the Knicks in the playoffs, star Scottie Pippin publicly disobeyed Jackson. He attacked the core of Jackson's team first philosophy.

Here is the situation in a nutshell: Pippin was told to go back with 1.8 seconds left in the conference semifinals. A frustrated Jackson finally said, "Are you in or out?" Pippin said, "I'm out." For some-one who constantly preached the team mantra, Pippin had thrown Jackson the ultimate slap in the face.

After the game, an obviously frustrated Jackson didn't speak directly to Pippin. He simply told the team: "What was broken was sacred. What happened hurt us. Now it's up to you all to work this out among yourselves. I'll leave you all alone to discuss what happened."

No one knows what transpired in the locker room next, but nothing like that ever happened again. Jackson said later that his job as a coach is to simply "help the team make music together, to create a format of harmony."

Another sometimes overlooked aspect of Jackson's team philosophy is respect for the opposition. He emphasizes that love must not only be shown within his own team, but that respect and honor should be given to the opposition as well.

"At a certain level, there's always a tendency to belittle the opponent, to break them down. We try not to overdo that. Honor the competition and remember that it is your opponents who make it possible for you to rise. If you tear your opponents apart, that hurts you in the long run."

Communication is a vital role for any successful coach. As a political liberal, Jackson was not happy to see Ronald Reagan win the presidency.

However he took away some lessons from the former president: "Eventually I realized what was so important and why Reagan was attractive to so many people. He delivered a coherent message people could understand and relate to. The leader's belief in a well expressed message can be more important than the message itself."

75. Military Leadership for Athletic Teams

The following chapter features an interview with Lt. Colonel JC Glick, former head of the Army Ranger Leadership Development School. He is now a leadership consultant for business and athletic teams.

How did your experience in the military impact your leadership philosophy? What specific concepts have you been able to transfer to your work with athletic teams that have had the most positive impact on performance?

In the military we wanted to provide our people the freedom to make decisions that were correct for the situation, we wanted to put our people through exercises that didn't micro manage them, but instead prepared them to take the next step in combat. We did that by putting them in pressure situations where they had to make fast decisions. We would allow them to go through the decision-making process and adapt to those choices, learning from the good choices and the bad equally.

We believe that if you teach them how to think instead of what to think, they will get used to thinking for themselves instead of waiting for someone else to tell them what to do. Much like the goal of a military leader is to create future military leaders, that not only are as good as they are, but better, I would say that the goal of a head coach is to create more head coaches. You also want your players to be extensions of your coaching on the field, not automatons that just do what you say when you say it, but read, think and act as a coach would. You want them to execute and process situa-

241

tions quickly instead of having to read and react.

How does that look like in real life?

You give them guidance and instruction and then prepare them to execute on their own. Questions to ask players to think for themselves include: "What did you see out there?"; "What is the other team doing?"; "If they do this again, what do you think we should do?". Those questions don't demonstrate weakness; quite the opposite is true. Those questions demonstrate confidence in you and your players.

I can draw parallels to fighting the enemy overseas. I wanted my team to describe the current status of any given situation they were dealing with at the present moment, and then be able to act correctly without my direct order. On the field coaches may ask their athletes to have "situational awareness" think it is the same to what I just described, but there is a difference between "situational awareness" and "situational understanding". Situational awareness is about knowing what is going on around you – situational understanding is knowing what is going on around you, knowing what it means, and knowing what to do about it. This is what we want as leaders.

If they didn't know what to do in a given situation, what did that mean to them and me? Two questions for both athletes and soldiers: "So what is our situation?" "What do we need to do next?" We wanted them to be adaptive and to solve their own problems.

Defining the culture. Making a culture deliberate. How can sports teams accomplish this? What are the primary roles for the coach and athlete to make this a reality?

Great cultures are built from the people up and then driven from the top down. The team should set the core values in context and the coach should make sure they and their players are living by those values.

It's important to avoid what I call 'bumper sticker leadership'. For example, a team may have a statement in the locker room that says, "Work hard every day." This isn't well defined and people from different backgrounds and experiences will look at hard work differently. There are competing ideas to what this means. So, it's crucial to define specific parameters of hard work means to the majority of your team. This context matters so everyone knows how to live by the values they establish.

Also, it's important to note that some of the players who may offer the most "push back" can also be some of your higher aspiration team leaders. They may have specific ideas on how things should operate, and when you give them a voice in the development of culture, they don't need to "buy-in"; it is their thoughts so they are "in" already".

To get more buy in, ask the athletes what they want. Also, ask them how negative actions by themselves or another player, or by you as the leader, impacts the entire team. Get them to think through how actions have a cause and affect on culture.

Come up with a culture statement. Who are we as an organization? This can be specific and generic at the same time.

Example: With the Rangers, we have something called The Ranger Creed. In this creed there are Ranger values, in context, that are both specific enough to tell you what your actions should be, but generic enough to have multiple applications. A line in the creed states – "Never shall I let a fallen comrade to fall into the hands of the enemy." This could mean carrying our Fallen Rangers over mountainous terrain to ensure they were safe. But it could also mean making sure someone doesn't have too many drinks and leaves the bar on time. The purpose was to look out for your brothers.

One of the rules is to, "Never lie to another ranger or officer." Sometimes you may have to lie in a given situation to protect vital information. However, you must always be totally honest with those you work and serve with.

Back to defining what hard work is. Does that mean 50 hours in the weight-room? That's obviously too much. When you ask an athlete what they think hard work looks like, they will most likely tell you (as the coach) what they think you want to hear. The key is to let them know there are no correct/incorrect answers. You can coax out an honest response using humor at times.

The key is to get players to discuss what hard work looks like. Keep in mind, an inner city kid and a kid from the suburbs might have different ideas of what a particular value looks like, just like people from all over the world see things differently. The goal is to get everyone in your organization to see each value the same and understand how to apply it appropriately depending on the context. Is 'thinking' part of hard work? Is 'looking after your teammates best interest' hard work? Just get players to use next level thinking to arrive at a common definition. Tell your players, "Hey, it's ok for us to have different opinions, but as a team we all need to see it the same way, and we will come to that consensus together."

The bottom line is that if it's not unethical, immoral, illegal, or unsafe, you can define your own leader principles. There are many ways to arrive at a common purpose through spirited debate.

From your time as a Ranger, did you do any beneficial team building activities that work well with sports teams? Describe one or two.

With the Rangers, we always worked as part of a team, the smallest being a two-person buddy team. The goal was to force people to problem solve together. The training involved creating shared hardships we had to work through together to solve. We would get a chance to rehearse what we would do together to reach solutions and solve problems.

Example: Let's say you have a tutor for study hall. Instead of a tutor mentoring the player, make athletes pair up and help each other out academically.

Example 2: Let's say you have a player, maybe a walk on who really excels at understanding the playbook. Instead of having the coach spend a lot of time on the ten percent of the team who can't seem to master what they should be doing X and O wise, have that walk on impart their knowledge to others. These guys can be like substitute coaches who can talk through everything they are seeing on the field.

Back to the Army. I would often have to test my Soldiers, and in some tasks the first go-round, maybe only 50 percent could pass. I would have those 50 percent teach the other half how to pass the test. When I used this method, it only took half the time for everyone to pass, instead of the full time of teaching them by myself.

Developing capacity versus having a top down culture of obedience. Can you share what a good culture versus a toxic or poor culture looks like? Can you give a few examples of what developing capacity looks like on a sports team?

It's easy to spot a culture that isn't working for the organization. Coaches enforce a culture of critique that often involves degrading statements toward players or athletes getting punished for the smallest reasons or mistakes.

The model for most coaches is that they will give their athletes solutions to common problems and obstacles they face. You teach them the 3 technique for example, they master it, and then you move on. That's a known solution to a known problem.

But what if an athlete is in a situation without such an easily solvable problem?

Capacity is the ability to solve a new problem when they don't have the answer readily available, or the coach there to ask. But you can't always control variables.

Example: A basketball player is taught to slide during man to man defense drills. Instead of the coach telling the players how to slide, he could take a few minutes to get the athlete to walk though how they would solve the problem for himself. A simple question like, "Where do you think the slide should come from?", "What about the second slide?" When they do that, the athlete owns the solution, not the coach. This builds confidence and leadership capacity.

Example 2: I worked with a pro football team and a wide receiver dropped a ball in practice. The assistant coach told him to place his hands in the proper position. But this is a pro. He already knows how to make proper use of hand position. Instead, ask the player, "What just happened to cause you to drop this pass?" Usually, they could tell you something like, "I didn't get my head around fast enough." Only when the player doesn't know how to describe what went wrong then you know they need coaching. Otherwise, you are over coaching.

So, let's say a kid messes up on the field. They come to the bench and the coach will either say, "You'll get it next time", which is kind of useless praise. Or they will tell them what they need to do next time in the same situation not to make the mistake again. This is better, but the best thing to do is to ask the player, "What happened? What caused you to make the mistake?' Then they can think though that and internalize a given solution.

John Madison, Editor www.championshipperform.com/books

Leadership is difficult. It is a lonely responsibility. The best leaders are servants. It is always about others.

DALE BROWN

SECTION VII

Fast Break Points — Second Half

76. • Practice Priority Exercise

From time to time, ask athletes to bring an index card to a team meeting where each person lists the top three areas the team most needs to work on. Compile the list and write the top 10 most common areas on a white board. Then ask the team of the 10 items listed what do they think the team should practice more or less.

You can state up front that the point of the exercise is to see if the players and coaches priorities for practice time are lining up. When they don't, dialogue on the reasons why you spend X amount of time working on Y skills.

• Peer Motivation Wall

Have an area in your team meeting space or locker room set where players can place hand written notes praising and thanking their teammates for jobs well done.

Simply have a bulletin board where the notes can be posted. A good spot would be next to a door on the way out of the meeting or training room at eye level.

Danger: Obviously you want to monitor the wall so that snide or disparaging remarks aren't posted. However, a few humorous notes are acceptable, but keep most of the content related to practice or game remarks.

Example: Sally was really unselfish today. She gave up open shot opportunities and set up two easy baskets instead.

• Recognize Team Spirit Award

A great way to motivate the players on your team is to annually give a "team spirit" award to the player who best embodies the essence of teamwork. You can have coaches and teammates nominate players who they believe is the most reliable teammate, who pitches in to help others for the betterment of the team, exhibits flexibility and grace under pressure, shows commitment to team over self and treats teammates with respect. The winner of the award doesn't have to be a star. In fact, giving the award to an unheralded player can often serve as a motivating factor for starters. Celebrate at a team dinner by giving the player a plaque.

• Women Toughen Up Practicing with Men

Many women's college basketball teams recruit men to help with practices. The male practice players usually serve as a scout team to prepare for upcoming opponents.

In scrimmages, the men will mimic the strengths of a certain adversary, such as teams good at hitting three pointers or scoring off rebounds.

The men's advantage in height, speed and strength give the women an extra challenge which coaches say helps them prepare for games in general, but especially against tall or very physical teams.

• Punish the Group for Bad Behavior

Do you have a discipline problem that can't get solved? When one player has a repeat offense, try this method to make sure it doesn't happen again: punish the entire team for the player's discretions. Make them all run, pick up garbage or some other form of punishment to get the message across that off the field conduct detrimental to the team won't be tolerated.

● Reinforce Team Vision

You can compel your players to dream big by asking them "vision" questions that will force them to articulate emotions, desires and dreams – which leads to behavior changes.

Examples: • "If we could eliminate one problem on the team, what would it be? What effect would it have?"

• "Picture where you want to see the team finish the season three months from now. What has to happen (other than wins and losses) to make you feel satisfied with our progress?"

• "If you could stop doing one practice drill, what would it be? What would you replace the drill with to make you and the team better?"

● 3-Point Goggles Power Up Shooters

You may have seen players making a strange gesture after making a 3-point basket. To celebrate the shot, players make an A-Ok sign over both eyes to form "goggles" with their thumbs and forefingers and stick 3 fingers in the air.

While the fad may seem silly and self-attention seeking, the gesture serves a good psychological purpose: it reinforces in the player's mind, they just did something well. The only downside is if they put too much emphasis on the gesture and forget to hurry back on defense. Other gestures like a fist bump after a made shot reinforces the positive outcome.

• Boost Team Egos with Awards Displays

You can award teammates with certificates and plaques, but unless you also display the awards where everyone can see them, you miss out on the full motivational benefit.

Focus on non-statistical awards like "Hardest working practice player of the week," "Best team player of the month," etc.

Here are the benefits:

• **Daily reinforcement:** All teammates will receive a daily reminder of the performance standards you want that reflect team values.

• **Improved motivation:** Team members will strive to earn similar awards so they can share similar achievements or see their name on the award board.

Strategy: Create a "bragging wall" in a central location – the locker room door for example. When players see hard work rewarded, even in small way, they will be peer motivated.

253

• Wooden's 10 Never Reminders for Players

1) Never criticize or razz a teammate.
2) Never be late for any class or appointment.
3) Never be jealous of a teammate.
4) Never expect any favors.
5) Never waste time.
6) Never make excuses.
7) Never keep making the same mistake repeatedly.
8) Never lose faith or patience.
9) Never sulk.
10) Never give yourself reasons to have regrets.

• Control the Team Meeting Dissenter

They are naturally combative, self-appointed devil advocates, or just someone is simply having a bad day. Some dissent is good and healthy. Other dissent is like a cancer eating away at team chemistry. Here are some tactics to keep in check all types of naysayers:

• *Look for merit in one of their points.* Agree with one thing that was said, but them move on.

• *Make light of their remarks.* Avoid sarcasm, but acknowledge their attitude. Example: "Wow, did you not get your coffee this morning?"

• *Toss the negativity to the team.* Ask how others feel by saying, "How many others share John or Kim's point of view?" That lets the team deal with the dissenter. If a good point is being made, then address it head-on right there.

• *Ask for a positive recommendation.* "You've given us a number of reasons why you aren't happy with the way we are doing things. Now I'd like to know how you would do it better."

● Kemba Walker's Dance Training Secret

NBA point guard Kemba Walker has feet that can take him any-where on the court in a flash and a body that can nimbly contort through a tangle of limbs. To top it off he has great timing and reflexes.

His secret: taking dance lessons since junior high. Squeezed in between basketball practice, Walker would take modern jazz and hip hop dance classes.

One of the dances was the Bogle, where the body mimicks an ocean wave. The dance background shows up in the way Walker contorts his body on reverses, shimmies his way through traffic and tap steps around picks. His has tremendous balance and his body is always under total control. That comes from practicing thousands of hours in both basketball and dance. If players need better foot-work, consider signing your team up for off-season dance lessons.

● Performance Coach Tim Grover on Injuries & Luck

• When the game is on the line, you don't want to hear "good luck"; it suggests you aren't prepared. When you head into a job inter-view, you don't need luck. You need to know that you are prepared and in control – not relying on some mystical intervention. Luck becomes a convenient excuse when things don't go your way – a rationale for staying comfortable while you wait for luck to determine your fate.

Top performing athletes rarely make changes just for the sake of change. What happens when you "shake things up" or "stir the pot"? You get random, unpredictable results.

Sometimes you will hear an athlete say, "Man, I just need to be surrounded by positive people." What that really means is that they want people who will lie to their face to make them feel better.

• "I once worked with an athlete who was attempting to make a come back after major knee surgery. He told me, "I just want to get better so I can get even with everyone."

I told him to repeat what he said again. Then I told the player, "Define even. He said, 'I just want to get back at all those people who said I couldn't do it.' Then I asked him: "Do you know what even means? It means you're equal to them. Side by side." Silence.

"Do you truly want to get even with everyone or do you want to get ahead of them? Why stand next to someone when you can get ahead of them? Go for the win, don't settle for the tie."

• Three Tips for Teams Who Miss a Goal

Use these three tactics if your team has trouble meeting a short-term goal:

256

Discipline and demand from your team without being demeaning. Shout praise. Whisper criticism.

DON MEYER

1) Don't allow discouraging attitudes to penetrate the team.
Remind team members that the goal wasn't meant to be easily
reached. Challenges make us tougher.

2) Recognize partial accomplishment. Especially with a harder
short-term goal, recognize small improvements or progress toward
that goal.

Example: If the team wanted to increase offensive rebounds 5 per
game but only got 2 more per game, pump them up by letting them
know they are almost halfway to reaching their goal.

3) Seek outside support. Find others with first hand experience
doing what your team is trying to accomplish. They may be able to
offer advice or encouragement. This could be former players or
you could find other teams and model what they are doing.

• Coaching Wisdom from the Movie "Hoosiers"

In the film "Hoosiers," Norman Dale (Gene Hackman) guides the
small-town Hickory Huskers to the Indiana high school state semifinals. In that era, schools did not compete in separate classifica-
tions based on enrollment. For this reason, Hickory's players are
about to play inside of the largest venue and in front of the biggest
crowd that they have ever seen. Just before the team takes the court,
Coach Dale addresses them with the following words.

There's a tradition in tournament play to not talk about the next step
until you've climbed the one in front of you. I'm sure going to the
State finals is beyond your wildest dreams, so let's just keep it right

there. Forget about the crowds, the size of the school, their fancy uniforms, and remember what got you here.

Focus on the fundamentals that we've gone over time and time again. And most important, don't get caught up thinking about winning or losing this game. If you put your effort and concentration into playing to your potential, to be the best that you can be, I don't care what the scoreboard says at the end of the game. In my book, we're gonna be winners! OK?!

The movie scene captures one of the primary duties of coaching: giving perspective to the team. Coaches foresee the thoughts and emotions that will be generated by an upcoming challenge. Then, they redirect the team's mindset away from fears and worries by reminding everyone of their strengths and focusing their attention on the task at hand.

• "Hoop Dreams" Movie Inspires

Teams are always looking for great sports movies to inspire the winning edge. One of my all-time favorites is a documentary called: "Hoop Dreams." Camera crews were given unprecedented access to the lives of two 8th grade hoop phenoms in the inner city of Chicago around 1990. They then followed each young man's life progression until college.

Even though it's nearly three hours long, the film moves like an edge-of-the-seat drama, brimming with tension and plot twists. There are ups and downs, triumphs and heartbreaking defeats. The off the court drama is no less gripping.

The movie begins as William Gates and Arthur Agee are being recruited by various high schools to play ball. The film allows the audience the experience of not only watching their journeys and daily routines (it's a sobering portrait of inner city life), but also witnessing their maturation.

The basketball games' film footage are riveting and your athletes are sure to get caught up in the drama (especially if they have never seen the film before). It's sure to inspire and generate some good post movie conversation.

• High School Experiments with Off-beat Method to Keep Athletes Engaged

A coach was having kids quit every year because they weren't playing much. He totally understood the situation reasoning that, 'if you can't ever play, why bust your behinds in practice?'

So he borrowed a concept from hockey for his basketball team. The idea is for each shift to play full throttle on the court, then rest while the next shift does the same. More than 12 players get into the regular rotation at his school.

They set the same goals every game. Some are easily met, others more difficult. They are as follows: 1) Take at least 90 shots or 25 more than the opponent. 2) Take half the shots from behind the 3 point line. 3) Force at least 25 turnovers. 4) Get offensive rebounds on one-third of all missed shots. This proves to be the toughest goal to meet. When all goals are met, the team is 32-1.

According to the coach: "I'm not saying this is for everybody. Basketball coaches, more than other sports, tend to be control freaks. I used to be like that, but now I roll it out and let them play more wide open. On game day, you have a diminished role and this is a foreign concept to many coaches. But I think it helps the players play more focused and full throttle at the same time."

• PHD Motto Leads to Success

For the University of Florida basketball team getting no respect proved to be the ultimate motivator they used all the way to winning the NCAA basketball championship.

The letters P-H-D stood for Poor, Hungry, and Driven. After being picked to finish at the bottom half of their division, the team came up with slogan as a way to motivate themselves and prove the "experts" wrong.

Head coach Billy Donovan had a signal he used during the tournament to remind his players to stay focused and on target. The team would look at him and Donovan would place his hand in front of his face and stare straight ahead. The message: don't be distracted with all the hoopla going on around you.

Besides staying focused, the other recipe for Florida's title run was simple: they played the game with a passion and unselfishness that some of Florida's former teams lacked.

The team's top four sophomore starters all shared an apartment and got along off the court as well. They lived together, ate together, hung out at the movies together, and occasionally danced together. They viewed themselves as brothers on and off the floor – their close friendships proved to be the foundation of the team's success.

● Mavericks' Secret Weapon During NBA Finals

The season that the Dallas Mavericks beat the Miami Heat in the NBA finals, they also won an overlooked stat. A detailed analysis of player-to-player contact revealed that the Mavericks had almost twice the amount of high fives, chest bumps, hugs or butt slaps. (These were totaled only by times done on camera, but the results were very definitive.) In the some of the games the Mavericks were 82 percent more likely than the Heat to give high fives.

The concept of team "chemisty" has been talked about to the point of cliché. But last fall, researchers at Cal Berkeley took a serious look at one of the most obvious signs of team camaraderie – touching. After reviewing broadcast of games from the 2008-09 season, they concluded that good teams tended to be more hands on than bad ones. Teams whose players touched the most often were more cooperative, played better, and won more games.

"I remember when we started with the coding, we were watching a team that was pretty bad that year. Just watching them we could see their negative body language and they weren't doing any touching at all – even in the first quarter. This is when we knew the study was going to work," said co-author Michael Kraus.
According to Mavs reserve Brian Cardinal: "It's all about positive reinforcement. We're a bunch of guys who get along well."

• Wooden and the Power of the Bench

According to former UCLA basketball coach John Wooden, "Too many coaches are afraid to use the bench. But it's the finest teaching tool there is. If somebody isn't going to play the game the way you want them to, you must put them on the bench. It doesn't matter how much 'star power' the player has. If the player isn't doing what you ask them to do, he or she isn't really your star player. True stars are the players who do their part for the betterment of the team."

• Wooden on Praise and Criticism

I told my players the same thing every year: "Fellows, you are going to receive some criticism. Some of it will be deserved and some of it will be undeserved. Either way, you won't like it. You will also receive praise. Some of it will be deserved and some of it will be undeserved. Either way, you will like it.

However, your strength as an individual depends on how you respond to both praise and criticism. If you let either one have any special affect on you, it's going to hurt us. Whether it's criticism or praise, deserved or undeserved, it makes no difference. If we let it affect us, it will hurt us as a team. You have very little control over what criticism or praise outsiders send your way. Take it all with a grain of salt. Let your opponent get caught up in other people's opinions. Don't you do it."

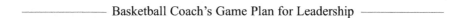
Great courage is not the absence of fear, but the ability to fight through it.

PAT SUMMITT

OTHER GREAT TITLES FROM
CHAMPIONSHIP PERFORMANCE

<u>World's Leading Publisher of Motivational Books</u>
<u>for Coaches and Athletes</u>

Read This Book Tonight to Help You Win Tomorrow

The Football Coach's Game Plan for Leadership

Total Athlete Development

Championship Performance Coaching 1 & 2

Control Your Off the Field Concerns

Good to Great Golf

Winning the Athletic Mental Game

The Executive Leader

Order online at www.championshipperform.com
Or call (980) 207-3288 or toll free 1-877-465-3421

THE
BASKETBALL
COACH'S
GAME PLAN FOR
LEADERSHIP

Made in the USA
Middletown, DE
08 September 2022

73012959R00149